STAGE BY STAGE

Richard Beer '75

Jean Scott Rogers

With a Foreword
by Donald Sinden CBE

Mr GARRICK in BENEDICT

STAGE BY STAGE
The Making of the Theatre Museum

London
Her Majesty's Stationery Office

© Crown copyright 1985
First published 1985

ISBN 0 11 290419 X

Design by HMSO Graphic Design

Printed in the UK for HMSO
Dd 718119 C70

Front cover David Garrick as
Benedick in Shakespeare's *Much Ado
About Nothing, c.*1770. Jean Louis
Fesch water-colour, indian ink and
gold paint on vellum.

Frontispiece Richard Beer. Pen and
ink drawing, 1975. The Russell Street
entrance to the Flower Market,
Covent Garden, to be the main
entrance of the Theatre Museum.

Relevant biographical details of
those closely connected with the
making of the museum can be found
in the Index.

FOREWORD

Two actors are said to have met in Charing Cross Road. 'Working?' said one. 'Yes' answered the other lugubriously.

'Is it a good play?'

'No'

'Good part?'

'No'

'Good money?'

'No'

'Why are you doing it?'

'There's a cake in the second act.'

All actors are attracted by the cake but very few, have concerned themselves with the history of their own profession. There have been notable exceptions. We can assume that when, after Shakespeare's death, his colleagues John Heminge and Henry Condell arranged for the publication in 1623 of his collected works, they actually had his original manuscripts in their possession. But where are they now?

The elder Charles Mathews in his time amassed a unique collection of theatrical portraits while his near contemporary Hans Sloane was collecting antiquities of a more conventional sort. Due to a powerful lobby Sloane's collection formed the nucleus of the British Museum but the nation failed to acquire Mathews's, thereby giving Britain the beginnings of a Theatre Museum in 1850.

However the theatre is never without its band of devotees and now, long behind almost every other country in the western world, Britain is about to open its first Theatre Museum. This book explains how much negotiation and persuasion had to be exerted in order that such a project should become a reality. Despite the hint of self destruction mooted in their briefing, the pioneers of this project had strong creative instincts and dedication which carried them through the dangerous field of battle and kept alive the concept which had been in the minds of theatre lovers for centuries. Their efforts have produced, by their sometimes ferocious tenacity against often unreasonable odds, a British Institution worthy of such fortitude and which one hopes will continue to develop by the very interest it engenders.

I am intensely proud to have been associated with the project for some twenty five years.

The list of illustrations in this book shines only a torch on the riches available in the spotlight of the museum. All the magic in theatre is revealed by glimpses of costumes, sets and the individual wizardry of actors and actresses. Nobody reading Jean Scott Rogers' account will ever take the museum for granted – nor the 'suicide squad' that formed it.

Donald Sinden
24th August 1984

CONTENTS

ACKNOWLEDGEMENTS

Since Alexander Schouvaloff first suggested, back in 1977, that I should write the story of the creation of the Theatre Museum I have become indebted to more people than can be listed here, but the following must be singled out for my grateful thanks: Lady Brunner, the late Constance Kyrle Fletcher, Dr. Duncan Guthrie, Laurence Irving, George Nash, Lord Norwich, Jack Reading, Alexander Schouvaloff and the staff of the Theatre Museum, Donald and Diana Sinden and Virginia Surtees.

I have also received technical help of a high order from Jennifer Aylmer, Julia Bellord, Hazel Holt, Lyla Osbiston, Anne Stallibrass and the late G.B.L. Wilson which has been of immeasurable value.

Thanks are also due to the Editors of *The Daily Telegraph, The Guardian, The Standard, The Sunday Times* and *The Times* for allowing me to use extracts from their newspapers and to André Deutsch, Ltd. for permission to quote a passage from the late James Laver's *Museum Piece, or The Education of an Iconographer.*

J.S.R.

LIST OF PLATES

They were to be a 'suicide squad'. Their brief: to create a national theatre museum for Great Britain then make their exit. Thus Laurence Irving to members of the British Theatre Museum Association when it was formed in 1957.

The following pages tell how the Association and other like-minded bodies achieved this object.

AUTHOR'S NOTE

PROLOGUE

WHO FIRST HAD the idea of creating a Theatre Museum in Great Britain? We know that as early as the sixteenth century Edward Alleyn, the Elizabethan actor and founder of Dulwich College, was making efforts to preserve theatrical material and that in the eighteenth century David Garrick and other men of the theatre – such as Charles Mathews, whose collection now hangs in the Garrick Club – had a similar aim. In 1871, the actor Henry Neville was urging the formation of what he called 'a Burlington House of the theatre', but it seems that nobody had the energy or the application to follow up Neville's idea until Gabrielle Enthoven began her struggle to find a home for her vast collection of playbills and London theatricalia. Her thirteen-year long campaign began with a letter she wrote to *The Observer*, printed on 10th November 1911: 'So many valuable collections of things theatrical have been sold and scattered that would have been of inestimable value to the student and worker of the Drama, for want, I think, of a recognized place where they could be safely housed and easy of access.' She advocated:

> a comprehensive theatrical section in an existing museum to comprise specimens of all the different branches necessary to the working of a play from the construction of the theatre, the designing of the scenery and costumes, to the smallest workings necessary in the house. Also a library and collection of playbills, prints, pictures and relics, etc. I want the section to be the place where the producer, actor, author and critic will naturally go for information, both of what is being done in this and other countries at present and what has been done before.

Her first choice of a home was the Victoria and Albert Museum. Here she received no encouragement. The Director, Sir Cecil Harcourt Smith, wrote to her: 'I fear the difficulties of our undertaking such a scheme are insuperable. I should have thought that it ought to form naturally part of the proposal for a National Theatre.' Gabrielle Enthoven was not one to be deterred by insuperable difficulties and her reaction to this rebuff was to seek a meeting with Sir Cecil. But he was away, and a member of the staff replied on his behalf: '. . . there is so little chance of your scheme being adopted that we should scarcely be justified in asking you to come here, as you suggest, in order to discuss it.' However, as has been said of her, she possessed 'that rate quality – tenacity' and she went on with her crusade in the national press, receiving publicity in *The Evening Standard*, which newspaper, at more than one critical moment in more recent years has spoken out effectively on behalf of the Theatre Museum.

In 1914 the struggle was brought temporarily to a halt with the outbreak of World War I, when Gabrielle Enthoven was occupied with War service. In 1922, with things returning to normal, the Victoria and Albert Museum devoted space to displaying theatre material assembled in Amsterdam in connection with the great international Exhibition held there that year. At the close of their exhibition the V & A bought certain of the works. This gave Gabrielle Enthoven the impetus to renew her efforts to get the Director to accept her material and in 1924 she succeeded. At that time the collection consisted of more than 80,000 London and provincial playbills, some dating from the mid-eighteenth century. Its acceptance took an Act of Parliament, which ensures that if the collection were ever to be housed in any other museum that museum would have to be part of the V & A. There is no doubt that this Act helped to determine the course taken in the negotiations for the Theatre Museum which took place in the 1970s.

How had such a collection come into existence? Gabrielle Enthoven is reported to have said: 'It was started when I realized that London was the only capital without public theatrical records, and I made up my mind to try and form one worthy to be accepted by the nation.'

Shortly after the Enthoven Collection had become part of the country's theatrical treasure, an article appeared in *The Daily Chronicle* under the heading 'Wanted a Theatre Museum – Stage relics without a fitting home.' 'Lovers of the theatre', it declared, 'have long cherished the hope that some day there may be a permanent Theatre Museum in London . . . If a theatre museum had been in existence it is quite probably true that Mrs Enthoven would have endowed it with her priceless collection of playbills instead of bestowing them upon the Victoria and Albert Museum. Here they are more or less a white elephant.'

The home of the 'white elephant' was the Department of

1 Mrs Gabrielle Enthoven (1868–1950), whose famous collection of theatricalia is now part of the Theatre Museum.

Engraving, Illustration and Design, then in the charge of Martin Hardie, and later under James Laver, from 1938 to his retirement in 1959. George Nash then took over responsibility for the collection, and his term of office saw the realization of Gabrielle Enthoven's dream when the Theatre Museum came into existence.

Once the collection had been removed from her flat in Cadogan Gardens, all expense of cataloguing, postage, etc, was met by the founder personally, and she continued to add new items out of her own pocket. She was the unpaid cataloguer and curator, and paid for the services of three assistants. That she had a sense of the dramatic (she was a talented amateur actress and a playwright) is illustrated by the hand-written entries which appear in the album she kept in her office: 'Work ceased here on declaration of War

Sep. 3 1939', and 'I started work here alone on August 13 1945. Gabrielle Enthoven'. In the interval, although by then in her seventies, she had been on War service again. After the War the Government provided her with a staff of two paid assistants, but she herself never received a salary. On her eightieth birthday in 1948 she was given a luncheon in the boardroom at the V & A by the Director, Leigh Ashton.

In his autobiography James Laver was to write of Gabrielle Enthoven:

> When she was ill in the last days and friends came to see her in the nursing home, she lamented to them that she was 'ruined'. This meant in Edwardian language that she would shortly have to draw on her capital. John Gielgud, with characteristic generosity, got up a subscription to defray her hospital expenses. When she died she left £20,000 to the Ministry of Education for the purpose of expanding her collection. Even this was not without its irony, for she decreed that, if the Ministry should refuse it, the money should come to me, personally. And I was the official who had to sign the form recommending the Ministry to accept it!

Gabrielle Enthoven died in 1950, aged 82, when it became known that she had once refused an American offer of £30,000 for her collection. Shortly before her death she became the first Chairman of the Society for Theatre Research. This Society, born on 15th June 1948 at a meeting at the Old Vic, had the aim of 'bringing together those concerned with the conservation of ephemera, theatre material generally, and with the history of the theatre, as well as the preservation of theatres themselves.' One of the begetters was Ifan Kyrle Fletcher, who was to play an important part in forwarding the movement towards the creation of the Theatre Museum.

In the late 1940s E. Martin Browne, Director of the British Drama League (now the British Theatre Association), founded in 1919 'to assist the development of the Art of the theatre', was proposing the setting up of a Theatre Research Centre at its premises in Fitzroy Square. The League feared – and rightly – that collectors of theatre material were finding it difficult to house their treasures and lacked a place where these could be held, and that students and researchers from this country and overseas had no centre where research could be carried on.

In January 1950 a meeting was held between the Society for Theatre Research, the British Drama League, the Arts Council of Great Britain and Westminster and St Pancras Public Libraries, to consider the setting up of a theatre research centre and library, with the hope that the library would form the nucleus for a national museum of the theatre. Two months later, the Arts Council called a special meeting 'to discuss the correlation of theatre material and the policy behind the formation of a National Museum of the Theatre'. Chaired by John Moody, then Drama Director of the Council, the meeting was attended by two members of the Society for Theatre Research – Muriel St Clare Byrne, its Chairman, and Sybil Rosenfeld, the Secretary. George Nash represented the Enthoven Collection. Although a further meeting was planned this did not take place and the subject of a national theatre museum lay dormant for a further five years. During that interval the Society for Theatre Research was engaged in organizing the first-ever Conference of International Theatre History to be held in London. It was this Conference which finally triggered off the movement which was to lead directly, stage by stage, to the establishment of the Theatre Museum.

STAGE *1*

EXACTLY FIFTY YEARS had passed since the death of John Brodribb, who called himself 'Henry Irving', and became Sir Henry Irving after Queen Victoria had dubbed him Britain's first actor-knight. Now in 1955 the moment had come for his grandson Laurence Irving to make his own contribution to theatre history by writing a letter to the press. At the time he was a Director of *The Times* and enjoyed the privilege of lunching in what was known as the 'Private House' of the newspaper's headquarters in Printing House Square. This house had its own links with the stage for it was built on the site of the first roofed-in playhouse adapted by Richard Burbage in Blackfriars in 1596. Laurence Irving tells how he discussed with the Chairman, Sir William Haley, the lack of a theatre museum in Britain – a fact which had been brought to their notice by the Conference organized by the Society for Theatre Research that summer. Both men agreed that it was anomalous that with the finest theatre material in the world we were lagging behind other countries in not having a museum where this could be displayed and archives stored for the benefit of researchers. It was decided that Laurence Irving should write to *The Times* pointing out this fact. Other interested parties were alerted to the plan and waited in the wings, ready to contribute their views once the Irving letter had appeared, for it was felt to be essential that any momentum this created should be maintained.

On 30th July Laurence Irving wrote, as from the Garrick Club, the letter which was to lead to the creation of the Theatre Museum. It was printed on 3rd August under the heading: 'A Museum of Drama – Need for central collection':

Sir,

British genius has expressed itself supremely in engineering, sea-faring, literature, and drama. At South Kensington, Greenwich, and Bloomsbury splendid museums contain all that is needed for research into the first three of these arts and sciences. For English Drama and theatrical history no such museum exists. The rich store of material in the country is scattered among a dozen public and private collections. Owing to the absence of a central authority whose concern it is to acquire the materials of our theatre history for the nation many treasures have left, and are still leaving, this country for enlightened foundations in the United States very much alive to the inspiration drama had provided in the development of culture in the English-speaking world. One such foundation has for many years placed a standing order for the purchase of Shakespeariana offered at our leading sale rooms. To-day any benefactor wishing to leave a theatrical collection or object of value to the nation is at a loss as to whom such a bequest should be made, none of the existing public or private collections being sufficiently comprehensive or coherent for purposes of research. The recent International Conference of Theatre History held so successfully in London is a reminder of our inadequacy. Is it not time that in the native land of the greatest dramatist the world has known and of actors and actresses of incomparable genius a theatrical museum worthy of them is established...?

Two days later a letter from Kyrle Fletcher appeared in *The Times*, welcoming on behalf of the Society for Theatre Research, Laurence Irving's proposal: 'a proposal which will fire the imagination of all who love the theatre. The Society,' he wrote, 'only has small financial resources but its 300 members possess energy, enthusiasm, and eagerness to work in the cause of the establishment of a British Museum of Theatrical Arts.'

Laurence Irving acknowledges the debt owed to the Society for Theatre Research. 'All too easily', he told me, 'sceptics could have dismissed our efforts in terms of the sentimental collection of relics of dead players, to be venerated like the bones of saints by theatrical devotees. The backcloth of sound scholarship provided by the Society was at all times invaluable in maintaining the prestige of the project.'

Following issues of *The Times* saw the publication of similarly supportive letters from Dr Richard Southern, Michael Nightingale, E. Martin Browne and Philip Gibbons (who was to become a member of the group of voluntary helpers who enabled the British Theatre Museum to keep its doors open in the lean years which lay ahead). The letter which appeared on 16th August carried the movement a stage further. Jack Reading, then Joint Secretary of the Society for Theatre Research, wrote that, encouraged by the response to the Irving letter, the Society proposed to convene a meeting of 'all interested societies, institutions and individuals', and inviting all who wished to attend to let the Society know. The Arts Council had offered the use of its premises for the occasion.

The meeting was held in the Great Drawing Room at 4 St James's Square, then the headquarters of the Council, on the evening of 28th October 1955, with Kyrle Fletcher in the Chair. Many of the speakers at the meeting were themselves owners, or were in charge of, important theatrical collections. In the course of his address Laurence Irving was able to report that the first financial contribution to the movement had been received in the form of a cheque for fifty dollars from Mr Jacob Wilks, an American citizen living in New York City, to be used without restriction to forward the aims of the movement. As one of these aims was to prevent the drain of theatre material to the USA the gift was not without its irony. *The Times* report of the proceedings contained a slightly sour comment. '. . . the discussions may be fairly said not only to have ranged over a wide field but to have made hay of it'. *The Museums Journal* of December 1955 printed a full account of the haymaking.

However, the meeting had one positive result: an *ad hoc* committee had been appointed. This committee met on 19th January 1956, with the Royal Society of Arts as hosts at the Society's house in John Adam Street, Adelphi. At this second meeting a sub-committee was formed, with the object of collecting evidence and exploring the genesis of theatre museums in other countries, and of preparing a memorandum on the proposal to establish such a museum in Britain. Duncan Guthrie was made Honorary Secretary and plans discussed for the production of a series of papers.

Among contributors to the original *Times* correspondence had been Virginia, Lady Clarke, wife of the British Ambassador to Italy, Sir Ashley Clarke. Lady Clarke had welcomed Laurence Irving's proposal, and referring to the existence of the Enthoven Collection, had asked the pertinent question: 'Since this collection already has the support of the Minister of Education, would it be illogical to approach the problem of official support – which will in the end be necessary – through the Minister himself?' But as was made plain in one of the Papers referred to above – *Sources of Revenue – No. 4 The State* – the sub-committee was against such an approach:

> It is reasonable to assume that the Government would be agreeable at least to consider an application for subvention from an institution such as the one we are discussing. We feel, however, that there would be little point in making an

approach until the new institution had become more than a scheme on paper – until, in fact, it had an existence of its own, with its own collection, of whatever size, with its own income, however insufficient.

At the time these words were written the committee was solvent – just: there was a balance in hand of £9.16.4.

On 26th July 1956 the Arts Council again hosted a meeting of what by then was calling itself the Theatre Museum Committee. This time the Chair was taken by Harry R. Beard, the owner of a remarkable collection of theatre material which, on his death, came to the Theatre Museum. Among other holders of material invited to identify themselves with the movement were Raymond Mander and Joe Mitchenson, whose well-known collection of theatricalia, housed in their home in South London, was widely used by researchers. They declined, but both partners remained on friendly terms at a social level and were to be seen at many of the previews to exhibitions staged later at the British Theatre Museum.

When the Committee met at the Theatre Royal, Drury Lane, on 16th May 1957, Kyrle Fletcher presided, and this time *The Times* was to report more favourably and said the spirit of the speakers had been 'almost Fabian in its dogged dedication'. A memorandum was circulated which contained the frank admission that it might not be immediately possible or desirable, to bring a Theatre Museum into existence. (Laurence Irving prophesied from the start that it would take seventeen years and this prophecy proved correct.) Meanwhile, the important thing was that an organization now existed to which people might entrust material in the knowledge that it would be legally held in safe-keeping. Four Trustees were appointed: Lady Clarke, Laurence Irving, Sir Michael Redgrave and Sybil Rosenfeld. A fifth had still to be found and his appointment was to prove of immediate benefit, for the man who agreed to fill the role was Seymour Egerton, Chairman of Coutts and Company, the famous four-centuries-old banking firm. Laurence Irving felt this to be a good omen, for it had been Angela, Baroness Burdett-Coutts, who had befriended his grandfather, Henry Irving, at a crucial moment in his career. Seymour Egerton invited the Committee to open an account with Coutts, and the Conference Room at its head office at 440 Strand became its regular meeting place until the start of the Bank's major rebuilding programme in 1973. On 20th June, at its first meeting the Committee elected Laurence Irving Chairman, Kyrle Fletcher Vice Chairman and Ivor Guest Honorary Legal Adviser, who had already prepared a Trust Deed and whose next task it was to draft a Constitution.

From the start this was to be a legally constituted body and this fact was to prove of value when the time came to create the Theatre Museum.

The next step was the creation of an Association, to be known as 'The British Theatre Museum Association'. The date of its birth was 17th November 1957, and this took place at the headquarters of the British Drama League. From that date it was to be the BTMA which held the stage, without official support, for the next eleven years.

Before the year ended the Executive Committee felt the urgent need to find someone to handle the increasing amount of material which was being acquired. In January 1958 they asked their Honorary Treasurer, Arthur H. Franks, then Editor of *The Dancing Times,* to invite G.B.L. Wilson, one of the magazine's regular contributors, to be Honorary Curator. G.B. (as he was always known to his friends), in spite of many other commitments, accepted. The appointment of a Curator was a relief to all concerned. Duncan Guthrie told me that all over London packages and boxes had been kept in cupboards, under beds and in every available corner of the homes of Committee members. What domestic repercussions this devotion to the cause may have had is not known, but it would seem that *The Times* phrase 'dogged dedication' extended to the families of those early members. In addition to appointing an Honorary Curator, when the Association held its first Annual General Meeting at the College of Preceptors in Queen Square, Bloomsbury, in December, they set up a sub-committee to advise

2 The Conference Room at the Head Office of Coutts Bank, 440 Strand, the meeting place for sixteen years of the Executive Committee of the BTMA under three Chairmen. This photograph, taken in 1973, shows (seated, left to right) Jennifer Aylmer (Curator), Jean Scott Rogers (Administrator), Ivor Guest (Vice-Chairman), Kenneth Garside (Vice-Chairman) and Lord Norwich. Standing (left to right) Sybil Rosenfeld, Jeffrey Archer, Major William Payne (representing the Royal Shakespeare Company), Jack Reading, Jack Deslandes (Hon. Treasurer) G.B.L. Wilson (Hon. Curator) and Kenneth Mackintosh (representing the National Theatre). Photograph by G.B.L. Wilson, (courtesy of the Royal Academy of Dancing).

the Trustees and the Executive Committee on the cataloguing and storage of the material.

All efforts to raise funds were unsuccessful at this stage, and the Minutes provide a picture of polite 'buck-passing'. Letters of Appeal were sent to many likely organizations but to no avail. Foundation A replied that it regretted it could not help but suggested an approach to Foundation B. Foundation B replied that museums were excluded from its terms of reference but suggested an approach to Foundation C – and so on. In spite of the strenuous efforts of Alan Jefferson, by then Honorary Secretary, none of the sources approached were prepared to make a grant.

STAGE

IN 1959 AT the beginning of its third year of existence, the BTMA acquired its first major archive and with it a boost to its morale. Laurence Irving reported that his grandfather's collection of theatre material had been bought from him, with the consent of the family, to be presented to the Association by a buyer who wished to be anonymous.

In the introduction to the biography which he wrote of Henry Irving, Laurence Irving tells how Tom Heslewood, actor and authority on historical costume, an old friend of Henry Irving's two sons, was also the owner of a theatrical costumier's business, and that after the death of H.B. Irving in 1919 he had acquired what remained of the Lyceum Theatre properties and wardrobe. Among the skips and boxes was a tin trunk, which he kept unopened until, shortly before the outbreak of World War II, when he was winding up his business, he broached what has turned out to be a theatrical goldmine. The trunk contained nearly a thousand letters written to Henry Irving. The trunk and its contents, which remained in Tom Heslewood's home in Hampstead throughout the war, survived the blitz to be presented to Laurence Irving, who says that the discovery of this correspondence was the 'origin and inspiration' of the book he then decided to write. When this massive task was completed he found himself with a collection of more than 4,000 items for, in addition to the incoming correspondence given to him by Tom Heslewood, he had himself gathered together press-cuttings, photographs, promptscripts and hundreds of other items relating to his grandfather.

The gift of the Irving archive was made public at a *Hamlet* dinner and exhibition arranged to publicize the BTMA, and held at the Saville Theatre in Shaftesbury Avenue on 1st February 1959, by permission of the proprietor, H.A. (Jack) Silley. Later Bernard Delfont took over the theatre and proved an equally generous benefactor. It was Silley who gave the Association its first shop window by allowing the showcases in his theatre to be used for miniature exhibitions. When he died in May 1972 Laurence Irving wrote a letter of appreciation which appeared in *The Times,* paying tribute to him, 'the first enlightened and generous patron' of the BTMA. With Jack Silley as host the dinner was staged on the opening night of the exhibition, and brought together a number of actors and one actress who had played the part on the London stage and elsewhere. Eleven Hamlets, including Miss Esmé Beringer, accepted the invitation and the event attracted a good deal of publicity. Kyrle Fletcher, himself one of the Hamlets, made the announcement that the Irving archive had been bought anonymously and presented to the BTMA. There had been a direct approach from a foreign theatre collection, which had precipitated a crisis, luckily averted when Laurence Irving received a 'completely unsolicited proposal which aimed to make the collection safe for all time in England, and at the same time to place the BTMA firmly in the centre of the stage of active existence' as a repository of theatre material. The anonymous donor, no longer alive, can now be revealed as Sir Felix Brunner, brother-in-law of Laurence Irving.

The gift of the Irving archive made it more than ever necessary to find a home for the museum. Meanwhile, the five cases containing the material had to be removed from Laurence Irving's home and put in a safe place as quickly as possible. The safe place was provided by Seymour Egerton, who made a vault at the bank available and, co-operative as always, allowed the Hon. Curator to have access to the cases so that bona fide researchers could inspect their contents, on condition that he stood by on all such occasions to invigilate.

Having played his part in the creation of the BTMA, Kyrle Fletcher resigned that year as Vice-Chairman, as it had become clear that his position might give rise to the idea that there was a conflict of interest between his antiquarian bookselling business and the Association in the acquisition of material. His resignation did not mean any lessening of support on his part and he continued his interest in the movement until his death in 1969. Sidney Monckton became Vice-Chairman in his place. Before the end of 1959 the Association had what was to prove 'a shot in the arm' when actor Donald Sinden was co-opted to the Executive Committee. From then on he and his wife, Diana, were to be deeply involved in the fortunes of the BTMA.

In 1960 the BTMA, now a registered charity, were negotiating with Neville Blond, Chairman of the English Stage Company, about the possibility of depositing their collection with the Westminster City Council, on premises owned by Westminster City Library. The Committee decided against the plan, but the negotiations had one good result: Neville Blond became a generous benefactor of the BTMA when what was called 'The South Kensington Site' materialized.

In April 1961 Lord Norwich was invited to join the Committee, and happily for the future of the BTMA agreed to serve. Alan Jefferson, who had worked himself almost to a standstill, resigned and Diana Sinden took over as Honorary Secretary at a critical moment, for it was then that a home for the collection became a reality. On the initiative of Committee member Antony Hippisley Coxe, whose famous collection of circus material was later to be acquired by the Theatre Museum, negotiations now began with the Kensington Borough Council for a licence to use part of Leighton House, Holland Park Road, as a temporary home for the British Theatre Museum.

Leighton House, a red brick Victorian building, now a museum and art gallery, was built in 1866 as a studio home for Frederick, Lord Leighton, President of the Royal Academy. An annexe, built in 1926 and known as the Lower Perrin Gallery, was offered to the Committee. Leighton House had been closed at the outbreak of World War II and was damaged in an air-raid in 1940. When it re-opened in 1952 the gallery became a children's library and this was its use until 1961. At first sight it must have seemed an unlikely setting for a theatre museum, far from theatres or other museums and standing in a quiet residential area. However, the Lower Perrin Gallery was conveniently situated on the ground floor and had its own entrance, and the Committee felt it was worth considering, although some members were reluctant to commit themselves. It was largely due to the insistence of Diana Sinden that the Council's offer of the gallery, together with two storerooms in Ingelow House in Holland Street, was accepted. Her belief that the time had come for a definite step forward to be taken provided the impetus needed. Like other Honorary Officers she went on to work herself beyond reasonable limits in the interest of the museum. That the Committee were able to aford the nominal rent asked by the Council was due to Seymour Egerton, who obtained a grant from the Coulthurst Trust, which was administered by the Bank.

Early in 1962 Sir Hugh Casson became Honorary Architect and Designer and produced two designs. His red colour scheme was adopted. In view of what was to happen later when the 'Fine Rooms' at Somerset House were agreed as the home of the Theatre Museum, it is interesting to record that Sir Hugh's design for the transformation of the gallery excluded all daylight. As a lover of the theatre he realized that theatrical material did not look its best without the help of artificial lighting, which was needed to give it glamour. By August the Committee were discussing the licence agreement which Seymour Egerton was negotiating for them with the Council, and in October the decorators moved in. The cost of turning the children's library into a theatre museum was borne by Neville Blond.

Up to now the Association had no salaried staff, all the work being done by members of the Committee, but Sybil Rosenfeld now recruited a group of voluntary helpers, the first of the many who were to help to man the museum during its tenancy of Leighton House. Lyla Osbiston, who had been helping Donald Sinden with his secretarial work, now identified herself closely with the BTMA, as did the new Hon. Treasurer, Barnabas Brunner, but it was obvious that a paid Curator and Administrator were needed to cope with the growing amount of work. Former actress Freda Gaye, by then Editor of *Who's Who in the Theatre,* accepted the post and started work on 19th February 1963. Diana Sinden was about to leave for Stratford-on-Avon, where Donald Sinden was joining the Royal Shakespeare Company, so for a time Freda Gaye was both Curator and Secretary, until Anne Suter became the paid secretary. By April, when Lord Snowdon accepted the office of

3 General view by Houston Rogers of the British Theatre Museum in the Lower Perrin Gallery, Leighton House, Kensington – the home of the museum from 1963 to 1977. The gallery had been transformed by Sir Hugh Casson from a children's library into an Aladdin's cave of theatrical treasures. Seen in the foreground is the Irving drum, once used to produce battle noises at the Lyceum Theatre, and converted at the suggestion of his grandson, Laurence Irving, into a display table where two-dimensional relics, such as original letters and programmes, could be studied by visitors through protecting glass. Behind the drum can be seen the bronze bust of Irving as Hamlet by Onslow Ford. Just visible on top of the filing cabinet is the *Chu Chin Chow* pot. There was no charge for admission to the museum, but visitors, if they wished to show their appreciation, put a contribution in this pot. It was in itself a museum piece, having been made on stage at His Majesty's Theatre during the record-breaking run of the Oscar Asche musical at the time of World War I. The firm of Wedgwood provided a skilled potter to make pots at each performance as part of the action of the show. The dressing-table-writing-desk on the left is claimed to have been designed by Sheraton for Mrs Siddons. The portraits on the ledge above the showcases are, left to right, Fred Terry, Ethel Irving (no relation to Sir Henry) and Ernest Thesiger.

President, material to be displayed in the gallery was being selected. To mount the opening exhibition a young artist, Joyce Conwy Evans, was engaged. She was assisted by Elizabeth Osbiston who, with her twin sister Jennifer, was responsible for mounting several of the subsequent exhibitions.

The opening ceremony was fixed for 18th June, and actress Vanessa Redgrave had agreed to perform the ritual tape-cutting. On 7th June disaster struck, one of the store rooms was flooded in a storm and much of the BTMA material affected. Drastic action was needed and forthcoming. With the co-operation of the Borough Council, the Curator, G.B., members of the Committee and the voluntary helpers set about the salvaging of the material and drying it off in the drained-out Ladbroke Grove swimming baths, lent by the Council in the emergency. To help the hard-pressed Curator through this crisis Diana Sinden came back from Stratford to prepare for the opening of the museum, and to deal with the press, who were beginning to take an interest in what was happening out at Holland Park Road. At a preview reporters were told that Leighton House would be used as 'a battle headquarters' for a militant movement determined to get Government recognition. For the present, it would concern itself only with the legitimate theatre, but when a national theatre museum was established other branches of the performing arts – ballet and opera among them – would be included.

4 Flood damaged photographs from the British Theatre Museum store drying out in the swimming bath, Ladbroke Grove, June 1963. Photograph by G.B.L. Wilson, (courtesy of the Royal Academy of Dancing).

STAGE 3

TRUE TO THEATRICAL tradition everything was 'all right on the night' and the museum opened at Leighton House according to time-table on 18th June. The guests, including the Mayor of Kensington and members of the Council's Libraries Committee, also members of the permanent staff of Leighton House who were to prove good friends to the BTMA, assembled in a marquee which had been put up for the occasion in the garden. Laurence Irving made a speech and Neville Blond handed to Miss Redgrave the original prompt copy of John Osborne's play *Look Back in Anger,* which was to become one of the museum's prized exhibits.

5 Vanessa Redgrave cuts the ribbon at the opening of the British Theatre Museum, Leighton House, June 1963, supported by Laurence Irving (Chairman), Keith Michell, Neville Blond and Tony Richardson. In his speech Laurence Irving said, 'How delightful it would be, if, when all else fails, Miss Redgrave invited us all to sit down with her in Downing Street until a Prime Minister gives her a Museum to open worthy of her genius and charm.' From the British Theatre Museum Collection.

The purpose of the first display was to call attention to the need for a permanent theatre museum, to be set up, as the press reported 'not by this or by any association, however active, but by the government'. In addition to this original semi-permanent display there were later to be twenty-two temporary exhibitions during the Association's tenancy of the gallery (see Appendix). On view on these occasions was material which the Curator would assemble, on loan, from other existing collections or from individual donors, and artefacts from the BTMA's own rapidly growing collection. The work involved in staging the exhibitions was felt to be justified as a means of attracting publicity and visitors, each one a potential donor or a new member. They also gave the existing members (by now several hundred in number) an opportunity to meet their Committee members, many of whom were conscientious in being present at the preview parties. The fact that the displays were often arranged to celebrate the centenaries of famous theatre 'names' gave them additional interest, while the presence of a well-known stage personality as 'opener' made them newsworthy.

A fact that cannot be overstressed in telling the story of the BTMA is that its intention was not to constitute itself as the national theatre museum but, by gathering together the rudiments of a collection and proving the worth and popularity of this to the public, to students and to theatre historians, to persuade the Government of the day to create a museum on a national scale.

Even as early as 1963 the material it was possible to put on display in the gallery was only a small fraction of what had already been acquired, and the phrase 'the tip of the iceberg' became an often repeated cliché when members of the public, on completing their inspection of the gallery would exclaim: 'Is this *all?*' Overseas visitors, particularly Americans, were astonished to find that England, the country of Shakespeare and possessing the finest theatrical tradition in the civilized world, had only one room for the display of its treasures.

Material had been coming in from 1958 onwards. Most of this was now packed dangerously tight into the two store rooms provided by the Council; the less fragile artefacts occupied one of the disused galleries at St Barnabas Church, Addison Road. Perhaps the most treasured single item, and by far the earliest, was a copy of the First Edition of Thomas Otway's *Venice Preserv'd,* 1682, once owned by the actor Spranger Barry (1719–77), with his autograph and hand-written cuts and annotations. A valuable influx of contemporary material came with the Royal Court Theatre (English Stage Company) Archives dating from 1956; the Debenham Collection of photographs, 1930–38, covering many now historic productions at the Old Vic; and the Cecil Madden Collection.

The museum attracted 400 visitors in the first seventeen days of its existence, although open on only three days a week, and by 24th October Freda Gaye was able to tell the Committee that the thousandth visitor had signed the book. From then on more and more visitors found their way out to Leighton House. Those from overseas formed a higher and higher percentage of the average annual attendance of between four and five thousand a year. The Visitors Books kept during the next fourteen years show that they attracted people from more than thirty different countries. From the earliest days after the June 1963 opening the museum offered facilities for research to bona fide students and theatre historians,

6 Dame Peggy Ashcroft and Donald Sinden at the preview of the British Theatre Museum exhibition 'Ellen Terry and her Family' June 1965. In opening the exhibition Dame Peggy presented the museum with this fan, which had once belonged to Mrs Kate Terry Gielgud, mother of Sir John Gielgud.
Photograph by G.B.L. Wilson, (courtesy of the Royal Academy of Dancing).

who discovered that in spite of the informal atmosphere the assistance they received was of a high standard.

Changes in personnel, both on the Committee and among the staff, were inevitable. In November 1964 Freda Gaye stood down as Curator in order to prepare for the fourteenth (Jubilee) edition of *Who's Who in the Theatre,* for which she was again to be the Editor. The Committee appointed Jennifer Aylmer, who had meanwhile succeeded Anne Suter as secretary, as Acting Curator. At the same time I accepted Laurence Irving's invitation to become Administrator. Within a few weeks of my taking office came the news of Laurence Irving's serious illness, which meant that Sidney Monckton took over as his deputy. On 18th January the following year the Committee passed a Resolution expressing appreciation of all that Laurence Irving had achieved in promoting the BTMA during his ten years in office, and from then on he disappeared from the stage. But only in a physical sense. Leaving the Chairmanship did not mean the end of his concern for the BTMA and he continued as a Trustee and to exert a valuable influence behind the scenes from his home in Kent. Lord Norwich became Chairman in January 1966. In accepting the office of Chairman Lord Norwich warned the Committee that he expected to be very fully extended for the next two years. He had recently resigned from the Foreign Office and was entering on a new career as writer and broadcaster. Nevertheless, from the moment he took office he was tireless in his efforts to get Government recognition for the BTMA. His first-hand experience of the House of Lords and the corridors of power proved an immeasurable asset.

By now further important material had been received, amongst it a large collection of Tom Taylor manuscripts; the Harley Granville Barker Collection of original manuscripts and typescripts; the Elizabeth Robins Collection; and Sir John Gielgud's collection of prints, photographs and programmes.

7 Ellaline Terriss, Ben Travers and Felix Aylmer at the opening of the 'Sixty Years at the Aldwych' exhibition, British Theatre Museum, November 1965. Ellaline Terris, widow of Sir Seymour Hicks, was over ninety years of age when the photograph was taken.
Photograph by R.B. Browning.

8 The Diaghilev Ballet Albums. In 1967 the British Theatre Museum received a priceless addition to its collection of ballet material when the residuary legatee of William Beaumont ('Monty') Morris bequeathed to the Museum six scrap albums which Morris had compiled during a lifetime of ballet-going. Many of the illustrations were cut out of magazines containing features on the Diaghilev ballet in its heyday and bought on the Paris *quais*. The contents are meticulously documented and make the scrapbooks of great value to researchers. Here Dame Marie Rambert examines one of the albums during a visit to the museum in November 1969. With her is Jennifer Aylmer, the Curator. Photograph by G.B.L. Wilson, (courtesy of the Royal Academy of Dancing).

Freda Gaye decided not to return to the Curatorship, so at the start of 1967 Jennifer Aylmer was appointed to succeed her. She took up her duties at a moment when the museum was seriously threatened with closure for lack of money. One of Lord Norwich's first tasks was to initiate an appeal for funds. In this he had the support of the press and the leaders of the theatrical profession. On 27th February *The Times* printed a letter signed by 'Dame Peggy Ashcroft and others' (sixteen years later Dame Peggy was still to be signing letters in support of the Theatre Museum during its recurrent crises). The writers on this occasion noted with alarm that unless relief of some kind was immediately forthcoming, the British Theatre Museum would have to close, and went on:

> The museum, which was opened in 1963 by energetic private enterprise, houses theatrical items of historic interest that would otherwise inevitably be dispersed. It is not only a source of enlightenment and pleasure to the public but a valuable centre of theatrical reference and a storehouse of irreplaceable dramatic treasures. This is not a case for renewed support by private generosity. We feel that the museum should be taken over by the appropriate Government department and maintained in a manner analogous to, for example, the National Maritime Museum at Greenwich. An estimated sum of £220,000 has lately been spent on an extension to the Imperial War Museum. At the present shoestring level on which the British Theatre Museum is run an equivalent sum would keep it going for 55 years!

British Actors Equity added its voice with a letter to *The Times,* which appeared on 8th March, in which the General Secretary, Gerald Croasdell, wrote on behalf of his Council:

> The closure of this museum and the dispersal of its contents would be a sad loss not only to the members of the theatrical profession, but to all those interested in the cultural history of our country. Surely, some help should be available from Government sources for the maintenance of this remarkable collection, which might indeed conveniently and at little cost be maintained, and if necessary re-housed, under the aegis of one of the larger museums, such as the Victoria and Albert.

Overdraft facilities had been granted by Coutts to the limit of £500, which figure would be reached by mid-March. In spite of a timely grant of £100 from Kensington and Chelsea Borough Council, the situation required drastic measures, and the Committee had to look around for ways to cut expenditure. Reluctantly they decided to economize on the salaries of the two paid Officers. It was agreed that I would cease to be employed after the end of

March, and it was not to be until 1st October 1968 that I was re-instated.

The man whose interest in the cause was now sought and who was to prove a catalyst was Lord Goodman, then Chairman of the Arts Council. He had not, up till then, visited the museum, but this was remedied on Friday, 3rd March 1967. He left saying he would call a meeting of all concerned and hoped that Miss Jennie Lee, the Minister for the Arts, would be present to hear the case for the BTMA to receive support. However, in spite of further discussions between Lord Goodman and Lord Norwich the Committee were told that no help could be expected from the Government at this stage.

Donald Sinden was also agitating for funds and seeking to interest Members of Parliament and others. Friends and sympathizers protested loudly but unavailingly, including Brian Batsford, Conservative Member for Ealing South and Deputy Chief Whip, who had recently been appointed to the Greater London Council, and who put before the House of Commons an Opposition Motion deploring the action – or rather the inaction – of the Government in not supporting the museum. The Association's original patrons, the Society for Theatre Research, were also active in their support, and the spring issue of their *Theatre Notebook* contained an appeal in which it had been pointed out that the development of the BTMA had been phenomenal and that it was ironical that it was this very development which had caused the crisis. 'This is not a case of an institution dying of inanition but the contrary. Its success has exhausted its financial resources . . .'

Practical help came from the Directors of the Wright Hepburn Gallery, Peter Wright and David Hepburn, who organized a series of auction sales in aid of the BTMA. In October the first of three sales held in their gallery in the Halkin Arcade, Belgravia, proved a boost to the funds to add to the grant of one hundred pounds it had received from the City of London. The auctions were a valuable means of keeping the museum in the public eye and had been suggested by the Directors themselves, as they specialized in the sale of theatre designs. Their generosity and that of the designers who gave their works for auction was a measure of the goodwill generated by the BTMA in the days of its hand-to-mouth existence, but the gesture cannot have done much to improve the finances of their gallery, which closed in 1971.

In January the museum had a visit from Mr Desmond Plummer, Leader of the Greater London Council, together with members of the Special Development and Arts Committee. This was taken to be a hopeful sign that the Committee had succeeded in gain-

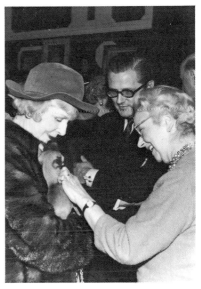

9 Lady Diana Cooper, with chihuahua receiving attention from Phyllis Bedells, who opened the British Theatre Museum exhibition to celebrate the ninetieth birthday of the dancer Adeline Genée, January 1968. Lord Norwich, Chairman of the BTMA, looks on.
Photograph by G.B.L. Wilson, (courtesy of the Royal Academy of Dancing).

ing the interest of bodies capable of influencing the Association's future.

STAGE 4

THE FORTUNES OF the BTMA were at a very low ebb when a parallel movement for the setting up of a museum of the performing arts was conceived. The man behind this new movement was Richard Buckle, writer and ballet critic of *The Sunday Times.* Richard Buckle has since written that when, on 8th February 1968, John Pope-Hennessy, then Director of the Victoria and Albert Museum, paid a visit to his flat in Covent Garden, he had asked him if he thought it possible that a future museum of theatre arts could ever become a branch of the V & A, and whether, if so, he would welcome such a plan. To both questions, says Richard Buckle, John Pope-Hennessy replied in the affirmative.

Covent Garden was in the news at this time, for it was about to change its character. The long-established flower, fruit and vegetable market was shortly to move to a new site at Nine Elms on the south bank of the Thames, thus creating room for new developments in the Covent Garden area. A day or so after John Pope-Hennessy's talk with him, Richard Buckle telephoned Jennifer Aylmer to tell her of his plan to form a 'National Museum of the Theatre, Ballet and Opera', to be housed in Covent Garden, and asked if she thought the idea might appeal to the Executive Committee of the BTMA. The Committee considered the idea an excellent one, which was hardly surprising as they had been working for the creation of just such a museum for the past eleven years, and said they would be happy to take part in any future discussions on the project. At the suggestion of Lord Norwich, seconded by G.B., Richard Buckle was at once co-opted onto the Committee. He agreed to serve, and later, at his suggestion, the Hon. Kensington Davison, who ran the Friends of Covent Garden, was also co-opted.

The following month Richard Buckle reported further progress. Lord Harewood, Sir David Webster and Lord Drogheda were all, he said, 'very keen'. The most important news was that John Pope-Hennessy was prepared for the Enthoven Collection and other theatre material in the V & A to be part of such a museum.

At a sale of Diaghilev ballet material held by Sotheby's in

September 1967 a quantity of costumes and front cloths had been acquired for Richard Buckle's projected museum. Now a second sale was arranged to take place on 16th, 17th and 18th July 1968. The events on the day preceding this sale, held by Sotheby's at the Scala Theatre, were in themselves high drama. In a Memorandum, later circulated to the BTMA Committee, Richard Buckle relates how Mr Antony Diamantidi, President of the Diaghilev and De Basil Ballet Foundation, having decided to put the material on the market, had arrived in London from Switzerland on 17th July and offered a sum of £25,000 towards the purchase of material for the proposed museum from the Diaghilev wardrobe and curtains if Richard Buckle could raise a further £75,000 that same afternoon. Richard Buckle tells how he got in touch with Lord Goodman who, with typical financial wizardry, called a meeting at his flat for 6 o'clock that evening – the evening of the sale. Present were Richard Buckle, Mr Diamantidi, Mr Gabriel White and Sir Max Rayne. Lord Goodman and Sir Max undertook to raise the £50,000 within three months provided Mr Diamantidi would lend this sum in addition to the gift of £25,000 he was making to the future museum. This was agreed, and the material, including the Picasso front cloth for the ballet *Le Train Bleu,* which fetched £69,000, was secured.

This sale was seen in some quarters of the press as a threat to the British Theatre Museum. *The Evening News* of 18th July suggested that it could 'knock all hope for the future from under the people who have battled to keep the British Theatre Museum alive for the past eleven years, and that although the Arts Council had consistently turned down the BTMA's applications for a grant, a trust – still to be established, but known to include the Arts Council with a group of sponsors – had spent nearly £72,000 on the purchase of costumes and backdrops which were to form part of another museum.' Asked for his reaction to the possibility of another theatre museum coming into existence, Kyrle Fletcher said he hoped that if this were so there would be 'some kind of amalgamation'. Which, of course, is what eventually occurred. It was clear by now that Lord Goodman was actively indentifying himself with the project. 'We must get a body together to get the museum under way,' he told *The Sunday Times* of 21st July, and this he proceeded to do.

A third sale of Diaghilev material, this time at the Theatre Royal, Drury Lane, was held on 19th December, when further material was acquired.

Lord Norwich was meanwhile pursuing his own line of action. Lord Rosse, Chairman of the Standing Committee on Museums and Galleries, had had his interest aroused by Lord Norwich's paper on the British Theatre Museum, in which he had made out a strong case for recognition by the Government. Lord Rosse had discussed this with the BTMA President, his stepson, Lord Snowdon. Both men were apparently agreed that a national Theatre Museum was a desirable aim, and felt that it would be excellent if a link could be established with the new plans for the development of the Covent Garden area. A pattern, it seemed, was at last beginning to emerge but it was to take some time before the different strands could be woven together.

It was soon clear to the BTMA that the aims of Richard Buckle's new body were identical to those of the BTMA. Ivor Guest, deputizing for Lord Norwich, had attended a meeting with Lord Goodman, Lord Harewood, Sir Max Rayne and Richard Buckle, and reported to the Committee in June (1969) that Lord Goodman's opinion was that it was unlikely that Arts Council or Government money would be available, and that the venture should look to private benefactors and foundations for support. The attitude of the BTMA, as summed up by Ivor Guest, was that they were in sympathy with the project so long as any new museum was established as a separate institution and not as a department of an existing museum. They saw no objection to coming in under, for example, the Victoria and Albert Museum. By now the BTMA had accepted the fact that it could not hope for Government support as a separate entity, Miss Jennie Lee having confirmed what she had told the Trustees in 1967 that she could not offer any direct Government support, and this was still the case.

By January 1970 it was clear that a new organization would have to be formed if the project for such a museum as Richard Buckle had in mind were to materialize, and Ivor Guest told his Committee that possibly the BTMA as a legally constituted body could be the instrument of such an organization. On 3rd March 1970 Lord Norwich attended a meeting at the Arts Council of what was by then calling itself 'The Committee of the Friends of the Museum of Performing Arts'. Although this body still had no legal existence, the meeting had been a watershed in that it had brought together for the first time in Committee representatives of the Arts Council, the Victoria and Albert Museum, the Royal Opera House, the Mander and Mitchenson Collection and the British Theatre Museum Association. At this time it appears that Mander and Mitchenson welcomed the idea of coming under the banner of the Victoria and Albert Museum, although they were already committed to a home which was being prepared for them in the National

Theatre complex. However, this home did not materialize, nor does their collection form a part of the Theatre Museum created in 1974.

November 1970 found Lord Norwich actively lobbying on behalf of the BTMA in the House of Lords, where he had gained the ear of Lord Eccles, recently appointed Minister for the Arts and Paymaster-General. As will be seen, this was to produce satisfactory results. In April 1971 Lord Norwich resigned the Chairmanship of the BTMA, signing the Minutes for the last time at the May meeting of the Committee, of which he was to remain an active member. The third Chairman of the BTMA, elected at the Annual General Meeting in June, was Donald Sinden, who had been an enthusiastic campaigner for the BTMA since 1959. In spite of being in continuous demand as a stage, film and television actor, he now threw himself, with characteristic gusto, into the task which he himself described as 'bringing the kettle to the boil' at a moment when dynamic leadership was essential to keep up the momentum created by his predecessors. He was later to declare that it had been luck which brought him to office at this turning point in the making of the Theatre Museum.

STAGE 5

THE COMMITTEE RECEIVED a transfusion of new blood when Jeffrey Archer, then Conservative Member for Louth, was co-opted in April 1971. He soon made his presence felt. In November he suggested that the BTMA might declare an interest in securing accommodation in Somerset House should space become available there after the proposed removal of certain Government departments.

Somerset House, an eighteenth-century building on the site of a former royal palace in the Strand, had been an early home of the Royal Academy of Arts, the Royal Society and the Society of Antiquaries of London, but at this time housed some 2,000 civil servants: it had been closed to the public for almost 150 years. *The Evening Standard* was running a campaign with the object of getting the civil servants out to make way for worthier tenants, one proposal being that the seven so-called 'Fine Rooms' in the North Block – which the Government by this time had spent £1,500,000 in restoring – should be the home of a national museum of the theatre.

By April 1972 Donald Sinden was able to report to the Committee that the possibility of the Theatre Museum moving into Somerset House was being discussed between Lord Goodman and Lord Eccles's department. A touch of drama took place at this meeting because, while this announcement was being made, Lord Norwich entered bearing a letter from Lord Eccles, who, as Paymaster-General, invited the BTMA to take the lead in formulating a scheme for a Theatre Museum and Research Centre 'perhaps in conjunction with Martin Esslin'. This recognition of its existence and capability by the Government came as a tonic and for a while a state of mild euphoria prevailed, although even at this stage there were some members who did not share the general enthusiasm about Somerset House as the ideal home for the Museum. The long-desired recognition had been achieved and such misgivings were not publicly voiced.

The reference to 'a Theatre Museum and Research Centre' needs a word of explanation. On 9th October 1971 a symposium, organized by the editors of the magazine *Theatre Quarterly,* had taken place at the Institute of Contemporary Arts under the chairmanship of Martin Esslin, then head of BBC Radio Drama. One of the objects was to discuss how best the movement for the establishment of a Theatre Museum could be given fresh impetus for the benefit of scholars and researchers. On the panel, as representatives of the BTMA and of the Society for Theatre Research, were Sybil Rosenfeld and Jack Reading. It was the latter who made the proposal that a new organization should be set up – a British Theatre Institute and Research Centre – to cater for the study of the contemporary theatre as a balance to the Theatre Museum which would involve itself mainly with the history of the past. At the time it was thought that the two organizations might work in conjunction and thus both were brought together to explore the possibilities of Somerset House as a joint home. In the event, as negotiations got under way, it was concluded that the proposed Institute should be a body separate from the Museum and this was confirmed at a recall symposium held in October 1972.

While all this time-consuming backstage work was going on the Committee found time to pursue another of its aims, namely the prevention of important national theatre material being lost to overseas buyers. At the end of November 1971, a collection of Sheridan manuscripts was auctioned at Sotheby's. These had belonged to the sculptress, the late Mrs Clare Sheridan, a descendant of the dramatist, and for this reason of direct provenance considered to be of extreme value. In the opinion of the Society for

Theatre Research and of Professor Cecil Price, the leading authority on Sheridan, the most important item was an assembly of draft stage scripts, annotated and corrected in Sheridan's own hand, of *The School for Scandal.* The purchaser at the sale was Richard MacNutt, antiquarian bookseller of Tunbridge Wells, acting on behalf of an American university. An application for a stay in the issue of the requisite export licence was made, and eventually granted, but the deadline for raising the matching purchase money of just over £2,000 was a tight one. Meanwhile Richard MacNutt had generously offered other material purchased at the sale to the Museum: this consisted of unpublished items related to the management of the Drury Lane Theatre under Garrick and Sheridan, all of great interest to scholars working in that period of theatre history. Jack Reading undertook the task of organizing an appeal to save the material and a press release issued by me as Administrator in March 1972 stressed the all-important fact that whilst eighteen acting scripts of *The School for Scandal* were known to be in America, not one was in the British Museum or elsewhere in the country.

Within days of the expiration of the export embargo, the manuscripts of *The School for Scandal* were saved by a donation from Sir Felix and Lady Brunner, matched by a grant from the Government Purchase Fund administered by the Victoria and Albert Museum, and sums from other donors. Donald Sinden had been an active campaigner, and because of his earlier connection with the Rank Organization was able to interest Graham Dowson, one of its Directors, and he in turn aroused the personal interest of their Chairman, Sir John Davis. This produced a further donation of close on £4,000 to complete the purchase of the additional material. Shortly after the success of this enterprise the National Theatre Company staged *The School for Scandal* at the Old Vic, and a display of certain pages of the manuscripts saved for the nation was arranged at the theatre.

In May 1972 the movement to establish a theatre museum was gathering in momentum. It was becoming obvious that although the Government might be willing to provide the shell of a museum at Somerset House there would be more than a reluctance to vote the capital and revenue money, with all the attendant legislation necessary for its establishment, maintenance and staffing. A solution seemed possible by a simple change in tactics: to make the Enthoven Collection, long-established and already a part of a state-subsidized museum, the nucleus of the proposed new museum. This innovation was tentatively aired and, by good fortune Pope-Hennessy, by now Sir John and still the Director of the

Victoria and Albert Museum, was in favour of such an amalgamation of collections. He confirmed that he would be happy if the BTMA could be brought under his umbrella, and was confident that the increased grant required to administer the increased responsibility would be forthcoming by inter-departmental negotiation. At the same time the hope was expressed that the protection of the same umbrella would be sought by the Museum of the Performing Arts which, although aiming to do precisely the same work as the BTMA, was still not a constitutional body.

Members of the BTMA attending their fifteenth Annual General Meeting on 7th June were not unnaturally anxious for news of developments, but the Chairman had to put a damper on their enthusiasm. He told them he had been advised that it would be improper for him to give them any details but assured them 'that the negotiations were proceeding in a very satisfactory manner towards a solution which he felt would fulfil the original aims of the Association', and asked them to have faith in their Committee for another few months. He felt that they would be proud of the result of the talks now going on with the other bodies concerned. 'The very exciting task which has been entrusted to us by the Government', said Donald Sinden, was just such a development as was conceived by the first Chairman, Laurence Irving, who had written personally to Lord Eccles when the news was first made public, once again stressing that, if and when satisfactory arrangements had been concluded, the BTMA would hand over to the nation all the material it had collected, without reservation and with no thought of self-perpetuation.

By October both Sir John Pope-Hennessy and Lord Goodman had been in touch with Lord Eccles and the proposals for Somerset House referred to the Department of Education and Science. On 28th April 1973 the DES issued a press release stating that Paul Channon, Minister for Housing and Construction, had announced in a written reply in the House of Commons to a question from Jeffrey Archer, that the Fine Rooms at Somerset House were to be placed at the disposal of the Victoria and Albert Museum.

Paul Channon's statement also contained the news that there was a possibility that the Fine Rooms would first be used in 1974 for an exhibition marking the centenary of the birth of Sir Winston Churchill. The probability that the Theatre Museum would not be the first user of the refurbished rooms was disappointing but obviously no protest would be in order against anything as prestigious as an exhibition in honour of Churchill.

The BTMA appointed a Planning Sub-Committee, with Jeffrey Archer as Convenor, to investigate the procedures for the merger with the Enthoven Collection and this was reported to the members at the Annual General Meeting on 12th September. Later that day an exhibition to celebrate the tenth anniversary of the BTMA's tenure of Leighton House was opened by Lady Brunner. Each succeeding year had brought additions to the BTMA collection, and in 1972 the John Masefield Collection and the Ivor Novello Collection had been added to the archives. Again, only a very small selection of material could be displayed in the tenth Anniversary Exhibition. Afterwars Sir Felix and Lady Brunner were hosts at a supper party in the Reception Room, at which the guest of honour was Mrs J.B. Coulthurst, OBE, one of the original supporters of the Association. In addition to Sir John Pope-Hennessy, civic dignitaries, theatre personalities, members, voluntary helpers and officers, were representatives of Beeby, Harmar and Company, who had been Honorary Auditors to the BTMA since 1959.

On 4th October Jeffrey Archer's Sub-Committee met Sir John Pope-Hennessy at the Victoria and Albert Museum to discuss conditions for the hand-over of the BTMA collections. It was agreed to drop 'British' or 'National' from the title of the new Museum; the time-scale of the operations was planned, and the question of staff considered to ensure the continuity of service of the BTMA Curator, Jennifer Aylmer, with effect from 1st October 1974. Jennifer Aylmer was awarded the MBE and went on to serve as a Research Assistant in the Theatre Museum until she retired in 1982. I had already passed the retiring age and would leave the scene when the Leighton House gallery closed.

Also in October 1973 Donald Sinden reported to the Committee that he had been invited to accept the chairmanship of the Theatre Museum Advisory Council, which would be set up in accordance with normal practice at the V & A. This body would have ten or twelve members who, according to Sir John Pope-Hennessy, would be asked to serve as individuals for their own interests and concerns, rather than on the basis of being the representatives of other bodies, although indirectly it was probable that such individuals would be closely associated with other bodies. Sir John, a believer in an active Council, said that non-attenders would be replaced. Bamber Gascoigne, Ivor Guest and Jack Reading, all three members of the BTMA Executive Committee, were also nominated to serve. It was explained that Sir John was in agreement for the new Museum to be set up as to be seen by the general public to be an independent entity and that it should offer the two functions of display and background research facilities, the importance of the latter being fully recognized. These arrangements were later to be reported to an Extraordinary General

Meeting of members of the BTMA so that they could be ratified for implementation.

On the larger stage, at the close of the year, Norman St John-Stevas succeeded Lord Eccles as Minister for the Arts and from that moment, whether in or out of office, became an invaluable ally of the Museum in the frustrating years that still lay ahead. Changes in the cast of the museum world had also taken place: Dr Roy Strong took over as Director of the Victoria and Albert Museum when Sir John Pope-Hennessy became Director of the British Museum.

STAGE

THE MEETING AT which the BTMA voted unanimously to recommend the Trustees to transfer the collection to the Theatre Museum was held at Leighton House on 6th February 1974. The resolution read:

> That arrangements which the Executive Committee have agreed with the Victoria and Albert Museum with regard to the Establishment of 'The Theatre Museum' at Somerset House be approved and that the Executive Committee be authorized to recommend the Trustees to transfer the collection of the British Theatre Museum Association to The Theatre Museum when that museum is duly established.

Jeffrey Archer told the meeting that the Theatre Museum would come into existence on the day a Curator was appointed.

The first advertisement for a Curator produced no suitable candidate, so in March 1974 a second advertisement was placed in the national press. As the result of this Alexander Schouvaloff was appointed.

As the Museum was not due to open until 1975, Alexander Schouvaloff was asked by Dr Strong to undertake some preparatory work during the summer of 1974, before taking up his duties in the offices of the Enthoven Collection at the V & A, (which had been extensively re-organized in 1970), on the day set for the creation of the Theatre Museum. During this period he met Percy Flaxman, one of the architects then working for the Department of the Environment, the body responsible for Somerset House, and made himself familiar with the various collections of theatre material which were soon to be in his care at the V&A and in stores up and down the country. Storage – always a Curator's bugbear – was to remain a problem for several years during which he was to struggle with the complexities of having material in no fewer than eighteen separate locations. This unsatisfactory state of affairs he managed to improve radically and the Theatre Museum holdings are now housed under one roof in a London warehouse. He learnt about the Enthoven Collection from the Keeper of the Theatre Section, George Nash, and spent some hours with a footrule in the Fine Rooms at Somerset House, measuring the available space and comparing his findings with the size of the collections which these would have to accommodate. Approaching the problem with a fresh eye it did not take him long to realize that essential storage space would be lacking in Somerset House. He consulted the DoE about the possibility of finding a building for this purpose in the Covent Garden neighbourhood, and was told that as the market was at last moving across the river the basement, or undercroft, of the old Flower Market building might be used. With the DoE architect he inspected the site and found that the area available was some 38,000 square feet, more than double the 16,000 square feet allocated for the museum at Somerset House. Here was a huge, nondescript area with no aesthetic or architectural features to hamper theatrical display, brick built and ten feet high, in an area with strong theatrical associations. Why not make the old Flower Market the home of the museum instead of Somerset House? Alexander Schouvaloff put the proposal to Dr Strong, who approved the idea, as did the Theatre Museum Advisory Council when it was consulted. But the question remained: would the Government agree to the switch of location? This required careful negotiation. Alexander Schouvaloff discussed the plan with the DoE and pointed out the restrictions which had been imposed on the users of Somerset House, among them the stipulation that the seven rooms should retain their architectural character which, in his opinion, made them unsuitable for a Theatre Museum. The architects agreed. The Fine Rooms were, in fact, too fine. So far so good, but opposition came from the Office of Arts and Libraries, who were footing the bill. The DoE was already committed to restoring Somerset House, but the Office of Arts and Libraries would only be paying for installing the Theatre Museum in the refurbished rooms. Any change of site would mean that they would be responsible for the whole cost of the operation, so, in their opinion, it was better to go on with the Somerset House project.

Whilst these negotiations were in progress the BTMA was preparing for the transfer of its collection to the Secretary of State. By 28th November, at a meeting of the Theatre Museum Advisory Council, Ivor Guest, who had prepared the necessary Deed of Gift, was able to report that he had completed the hand-over of the collection. One of the effects of the transfer was that from this time the DoE took over the responsibility of the museum at Leighton House and paid the rates on the storerooms, whilst the Department of Education and Science took over the running expenses.

When Alexander Schouvaloff, by now a member of the BTMA Committee, attended their meeting in March 1975 he reported that the Theatre Museum Advisory Council had seen both sites – Somerset House and the Flower Market building in Covent Garden – and had written advising the Minister that they considered the latter a more suitable place. The GLC were now known to favour the idea of having the Theatre Museum in Covent Garden, and were initiating talks with the DES. The main objection to the Flower Market site was, he told them, cost. He described the restrictions on display which would make a Theatre Museum in Somerset House almost impossible, and told the Committee that various people had been trying to force the lobby for the alternative to be considered by the Minister. At the request of the Committee he arranged for them to see the Covent Garden site.

One of the bodies lobbying for Covent Garden to be considered was the Turner lobby. The successful J.M.W. Turner Exhibition at Burlington House (autumn 1974 to spring 1975) had produced a group of influential people campaigning for a permanent home for the display of the painter's works in Somerset House. Among them were the Poet Laureate Sir John Betjeman and the sculptor Henry Moore. Alexander Schouvaloff had realized the importance of gaining their support for the plan to change the site of the Theatre Museum from Somerset House to Covent Garden. After a meeting with Sir John, who was immediately sympathetic, Mrs Vera Russell, an active member of the Turner lobby, arranged a meeting

10 Exterior of the old Flower Market building, Covent Garden, Spring 1975. G.B.L. Wilson, Hon. Curator of the British Theatre Museum, with Alexander Schouvaloff, Curator of the Theatre Museum, outside the future home of the museum where work on conversion finally started on 30th January 1984.
Photograph by G.B.L. Wilson, (courtesy of the Royal Academy of Dancing).

at County Hall to air the subject with the GLC. Both the Leader and Deputy Leader of the GLC were present, as was Henry Moore, and the meeting resulted in the GLC expressing themselves as in favour of putting the Theatre Museum into the Flower Market. This was a move in the right direction, but the Office of Arts and Libraries had still to be won over.

On 2nd February 1975 *The Sunday Times* quoted Dr Strong on the subject of Somerset House as a home for the Theatre Museum. He was not at all sure about its being the ideal place, but that 'No one had regarded Somerset House as the last resting home of the theatre museum. It is an interim solution. The final resting place won't come in my lifetime.' The same article reported Alexander Schouvaloff as being of the opinion that 'The beautiful rooms,with their eighteenth-century painted and stucco ceilings and huge windows, are not the appropriate place for a theatre museum. What is needed is a soundproof dark box to conjure up the magic of the theatre.'

Public spending cuts were now the order of the day, and so negotiations flagged. It had been realised by this time that the museum could not have opened at the end of 1975 at Somerset House as had been hoped. Going to the Flower Market, if the Government agreed to the change of site, would delay the opening still further. If they agreed, the DoE architects would be responsible for the basic work of planning the fire exits, lavatories, and for removing unwanted partitions, but the museum itself had to be designed. A Consultant Architect was needed, someone with experience of staging exhibitions, who was at the same time a qualified architect, and in sympathy with the project. Alexander Schouvaloff's proposal to appoint John Paterson of Edinburgh met with the approval of the Property Services Agency, and on him now fell the task of preparing plans to transform the Flower Market building. This operation had to be treated as one: the Theatre Museum being responsible for displaying the objects, the PSA for planning the area where they would be displayed.

When Alexander Schouvaloff was introduced to members of the BTMA at their eighteenth Annual General Meeting on 3rd June, he told them that more suitable premises had become available for the Theatre Museum and that the Minister for the Arts had agreed to consider the alternative of the old Flower Market in Covent Garden. A feasibility study had been carried out, which showed that the cost of putting the Theatre Museum into Covent Garden would not be much greater, although air-conditioning would have to be installed in the basement.

At the same meeting Ivor Guest, as Chairman of the BTMA

Working Party for the Friends of the Theatre Museum, which it was hoped would eventually take the place of the BTMA, told members that a Memorandum and Articles of Association had been drafted and would shortly be discussed with the V & A. The new organization (later to be re-named the Theatre Museum Association) was intended as a purpose-built body with the aim of stimulating interest in the Theatre Museum, assisting its work in a variety of ways, including the making of grants for purchases.

The news that the Government had agreed that the Flower Market would be the new home of the Theatre Museum was announced on the radio and in the press on 5th September 1975. An unofficial estimate gave the probable opening date as late 1977 or early 1978.

Those concerned with the care of the 20,000 books and periodicals which will form an important feature of the Theatre Museum were among those most relieved by the Government announcement, for the Flower Market would afford greater space for a library. The library consists of the collections brought together from the Harry R. Beard Theatre Collection; the Cyril Beaumont Collection; the British Theatre Museum Collection, which includes the Irene Mawer Memorial Library (chiefly works on the art of mime); the Enthoven Collection; the London Archives of the Dance; the Society for Theatre Research Collection and the Vic-Wells Library from the Old Vic. The work of cataloguing and classifying the growing number of works is in the hands of Dorothy Moore, assisted by a retired librarian, Dorothy Procter, both in a voluntary capacity. Dr James Fowler, Assistant Curator of the Theatre Museum, told me that he expects the Theatre Museum Reference Library to be 'a library of first resort where research will start, as well as one of last resort, frequented by those pursuing obscure works which even the British Library may not have.'

Financial concern was the dominating feature of 1976. When Alexander Schouvaloff reported to the BTMA Committee in July he told them that the Theatre Museum had entered a new financial year and that the situation was a great deal worse than it had been in the previous year. No increase in the budget would be possible for the moment. There would, in fact, probably have to be cuts in expenditure, and there was no chance of taking on any extra staff before the move to Covent Garden. It was hoped that the lease of the premises would be signed in September, when 'approvals' had been received, after which date the DoE would rent the building from the GLC. Meanwhile, the architects were working on their plans and it was expected that a start could be made on the actual building operations towards the end of 1977, and the major part completed in 1978. At this time he was still optimistic enough to think that 1979 could stand as the opening date.

The curtain was still up at Leighton House, where I had been put in charge, helped by such volunteers as were available, and the museum remained open to the public on three days a week. We were preparing for a Christmas party, planned before the economic wind had begun to blow cold, when Alexander Schouvaloff was to give members a progress report on the conversion work at Covent Garden. Instead, he had to report a serious financial setback. It seemed that the DoE would not be able to provide the necessary funds for transforming the building before 1984. His plan now was to try and raise £50,000 to £80,000 from the private sector within the next six months or so. His news put a damper on the festivities. However, early in 1977 the DoE and the DES announced that they would provide £350,000 over the period 1978, 1979 and 1980, and that an official statement to this effect would be made in the House of Lords shortly. Work could now start on the site in July 1978, and the museum would open two years later. Once again the Committee heaved a corporate sigh of relief and the minutes record that 'Mr Schouvaloff's report was received with great satisfaction.'

STAGE 7

IT WAS IN February 1977 that the Hon. Treasurer, by now Jack Deslandes, reported that the BTMA had not the funds to carry on until the Theatre Museum opened in 1984. The annual subscription barely covered the cost of stationery and postage, but no increase could be contemplated as there was no inducement to members to pay a higher subscription, nor could the Working Party for the Friends of the Theatre Museum advance farther, as the delays over the Covent Garden premises meant that there was no possibility of a successful drive for members without something tangible to offer them. The Committee had to face reality and set about dissolving the BTMA. According to its constitution this involved the passing of a resolution to dissolve, passed by a plain majority of members, and then confirmed at a second meeting to be held not less than a month after the Annual General Meeting, when members could vote either in person or by proxy. This Extraordinary General Meeting was held at Leighton House on 30th September 1977 when the resolution was confirmed: 'That the British Theatre Museum Association be dissolved on 30th September, 1977, and that its assets be transferred to The Friends of The Theatre Museum, Limited.'

The Committee had met for the last time at King's College, Strand, on 22nd June, and all that remained for me to do was to plan a Final Gathering of BTMA members and friends at Leighton House. After twenty years campaigning for a national theatre museum, the Association can truly be said to have been dissolved with a bang rather than a whimper. On the afternoon of Saturday, 12th November, the weather staged it own spectacular, with a mighty rushing wind, thunder, lightning and even a snow flurry for good measure. Fortunately the most violent of these effects occurred after the completion of the ceremony in the garden. For this the audience stood around, warmly clad, ankle-deep in drifts of fallen leaves and listened to speeches from Donald Sinden and Lady Brunner, who then unveiled a plaque at the foot of a young cherry tree planted 'to commemorate the foundation of the British Theatre Museum which from 1963 had its first home in Leighton House.'

The museum remained open until 29th December, when the curtain was metaphorically rung down. The doors having been locked on the last visitors at 17.00 hours, Alexander Schouvaloff produced champagne to mark the moment when Jennifer Aylmer and I formally handed over the keys. The gallery was from then on

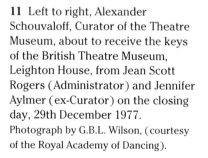

11 Left to right, Alexander Schouvaloff, Curator of the Theatre Museum, about to receive the keys of the British Theatre Museum, Leighton House, from Jean Scott Rogers (Administrator) and Jennifer Aylmer (ex-Curator) on the closing day, 29th December 1977.
Photograph by G.B.L. Wilson, (courtesy of the Royal Academy of Dancing).

used for storage and cataloguing until it reverted to the Borough Council, and within a short space of time all traces of the BTMA were obliterated. Laurence Irving's 'suicide squad' had fulfilled its objective, even if not quite in the way foreseen by its founders in 1957. Several of its leading members, including Ivor Guest, Lord Norwich, Jack Reading and Donald Sinden continued, however, to fight in the battles for the survival of the Theatre Museum they had helped to create.

A setback occurred in 1978 when work in connection with the London Transport Museum, which was to be housed on the ground floor of the old Flower Market building, was in progress. The glass had been removed from the roof and the task of sand-blasting with water all the Victorian painted ironwork put in hand. Stanchions had been inserted in the floor, which was, of course, the ceiling of the future Theatre Museum. These stanchions let in water and, coinciding with a period of heavy rainfall, caused saturation of the walls of the undercroft. This massive saturation was such that it would have cost £50,000 to dry off mechanically, so the alternative – to leave the walls to dry naturally over the course of a year – was accepted in the absence of the Office of Arts and Libraries giving formal approval for the expenditure.

In 1979 Norman St John-Stevas became Minister for the Arts. At that time the Theatre Museum was told to go ahead, and when Paul Channon succeeded him as Minister this was still the case. But in May 1982 a crisis occurred when Gordon Burrett came in to investigate the Departmental Museums – the V&A, the Science Museum and the Museum of Childhood – as part of what came to be known as the 'Rayner Scrutiny' ordered by the Prime Minister. The Burrett Report included among its recommendations the devolution of the V & A, a recommendation accepted by the Minister to the satisfaction of Sir Roy Strong, who had long wished for a Trustee Museum. But it also recommended the abandonment of the Theatre Museum, obviously considered as a luxury not to be contemplated under present economic conditions.

Things looked black for the survival of the museum. Alexander Schouvaloff immediately organized a vigorous campaign, sending out a spate of letters to public and private people both in this country and abroad, urging them to write to the Minister for the Arts protesting against the intention to abandon the Theatre Museum. The response was overwhelming. Many people were ready and willing to co-operate, including the theatrical establishment, led again by Dame Peggy Ashcroft, this time with the support of Sir Claus Moser, with a letter to *The Times*. The press generally, and Louis Kirby, Editor of *The Standard,* particularly, was loud in its support. Over 2,000 men and women of standing responded to the appeal and wrote to the Minister – heartening evidence of the goodwill which the Theatre Museum had already generated.

Two petitions were started, one of these by *The Standard* and the other by the Theatre Museum Association. For the Association's petition Richard Buckle secured the help of artist David Hockney, who gave a drawing of a Commedia del'Arte-type clown,

12 Smiley the clown, who helped in getting signatures to the Theatre Museum petition, during the week in Covent Garden. He is wearing a Theatre Museum T-shirt and brandishing *The Standard* announcement of the 15,000 signatures collected in its campaign to save the museum. Photograph by Andrew Bridge.

which was reproduced on a leaflet with a tear-off strip at the foot for protesters against the shelving of the museum to sign. Between them the two petitions produced more than 32,000 signatures. On 22nd July the package was delivered to Paul Channon's office by a group of actors, headed by Paul Eddington. The weight of evidence in support of the museum convinced the Minister, and by 11th August the battle had been won: the Theatre Museum was reprieved. It took this crisis to provide proof that the British public was behind it.

In the autumn of 1982 Liberty of Regent Street came to Alexander Schouvaloff with the news that they were to be hosts to the Silk Commission, and invited the Theatre Museum to organize an exhibition of silk costumes to be held on their premises. The exhibition, arranged by Philip Dyer, received helpful publicity and the midnight supper party given by Liberty's on 20th September was a means of repaying many of the people who had helped in the campaign to save the museum.

Paper work on the Flower Market, stopped in May, now began again. Working drawings and bills of quantities were to be completed by the end of September. The documents had been sent out and tenders were to be in before Christmas, but there were still delays on the lease negotiations. Paul Channon reiterated that the actual work of converting the building would start either in January or March 1983. But there was another delay, and the lease finally was to be exchanged on Friday 8th July, then changed to 7th July. On the 7th the new Minister for the Arts, the Earl of Gowrie, appointed when the Conservatives were returned to power in the General Election of 9th June, announced the shelving of the Theatre Museum as part of the drastic cuts in Government expenditure required by the new Chancellor of the Exchequer, Nigel Lawson.

Sir Roy Strong, who had only been told of the plan to shelve the museum a few hours before the official statement, telephoned Alexander Schouvaloff to let him know what had happened, and he in his turn had the unenviable task of breaking the news to his staff. The statement came as a severe shock, but the Government, who were looking for ways of reducing expenditure, must have had the Theatre Museum in their minds as a possible victim for some time. The news made front-page headlines in the national press. *The Standard* quoted Sir Roy as saying he would act on the assumption that the Theatre Museum was likely to remain in its present quarters at the Victoria and Albert Museum 'for the foreseeable future'. *The Guardian* quoted him as saying: 'This is a setback but as anyone who has anything to do with show business

13a A corner of 'Spotlight' – an innovative exhibition of four centuries of ballet costume, including a tribute to the Royal Ballet, staged at the Victoria and Albert Museum, April 1981, using the new microchip technology for the control of sound and light. The soundtrack included pulses for the lighting sequence so that the rhythm of the music was matched to the changes of light. Designed by John L. Paterson, with display by Philip Dyer and Judith Doré.

13b HRH The Princess Margaret, Countess of Snowdon, at the opening of the 'Spotlight' exhibition. With Her Royal Highness in the photograph are, left to right, Lady Strong (Julia Trevelyan Oman), Mrs Alexander Schouvaloff, Sir Roy Strong, Richard Buckle and Mrs Helen Stubbs.

knows the curtain must go up and the show will go on here as before.' The press could collect no quote from Alexander Schouvaloff: he was still a civil servant, although as a result of the Burrett Report, the V & A had been devolved from the DES since May and was now a Trustee Museum under the Chairmanship of Lord Carrington.

Among those who said they were 'deeply shocked' by the Chancellor's announcement was Norman St John-Stevas, who had supported the museum during the crisis in 1982. He now declared that the theatre world should act to ensure that the museum went ahead as planned, whilst he himself organized a delegation to wait on Lord Gowrie. Lord Strabolgi, Labour spokesman on the Arts in the House of Lords, also took prompt action and arranged an emergency debate for 12th July. He said the decision to shelve the museum was scandalous: 'I think it is a breach of faith with the very generous donors and people who have left bequests to the museum.' As in the 1982 crisis, reactions to the news both from Right and Left proved that the Theatre Museum had good friends in the Government and amongst the Opposition.

From the first day of this new crisis *The Standard* was loud in its

14 British ballerina Dame Alicia Markova, with (left) Alexander Schouvaloff, Curator of the Theatre Museum, and (right) Ballet and Dance Consultant Philip Dyer, when Dame Alicia presented fourteen tutus from her collection of ballet costumes to the Museum, April 1983.

15 HRH The Princess Margaret, with Lord Snowdon and the Countess of Rosse and Sir Roy Strong, at the Private View Party at which Her Royal Highness opened the Oliver Messel Exhibition at the Victoria and Albert Museum, June 1983.

support. In an article published on 11th July it declared:

> How mean! The Theatre Museum is not a toy that this Government can set up and destroy at will like a child in a nursery! As last year's *Standard* campaign made plain, it is an important showcase of a vital part of British culture, and one which is long overdue . . . Less than a year ago the Government accepted this argument when it gave the museum in Covent Garden the go-ahead. Now, in a decision that is as cruel as it is miserly, it has withdrawn funding just as it was about to exchange a lease with the GLC. For a mere £4,000,000 – a drop in the ocean as regards its public spending budget – it has reneged on a firm commitment!

On 12th July it printed a blunt statement from Sir Roy Strong, who said the future of the Theatre Museum had reached the make or break stage.

> We cannot go on like this. Unless there is a specific pledge to make the money available I will go to my board of Trustees and recommend that everything that has been collected for the Theatre Museum should be returned to its owners. We are

acting under false pretences if we retain artefacts that have been given to the nation and do not place them on display.

On 18th July *The Times* printed yet another letter signed by Dame Peggy Ashcroft, Sir John Gielgud and others:

We were very relieved when, in August 1982, the announcement was made that the Theatre Museum should go ahead as planned in Covent Garden 'with all possible speed', and that former promises were to be honoured at last. We assumed that building was under way. How wrong we were. The cut announced last week is a betrayal of all those who have given to the Museum and of all those who fought so hard to save it successfully last year. The fact that the cut was announced on the eve of exchanging the lease with the GLC smacks of very sharp practice. We do not want further promises about next year. We trust that the Government will immediately reverse its decision about the Theatre Museum, allow it to go ahead now and be seen to have kept its word.

On 27th July *The Standard* reported that the Government and the GLC had met to discuss new terms of the lease on the old Flower Market building. On 1st August it was announced that a private donor, described by the Minister for the Arts as 'an angel who has decided to blush unseen' had saved the museum. It was Tony Banks, the GLC Arts Committee Chairman, who had suggested to the Minister 'an alteration to the usual form of the lease agreement, allowing the Government to commit itself once and for all to the scheme, but with a delayed start on the conversion work'. Sir Roy Strong was quoted as having congratulated the Minister on what he called 'this brilliant coup'. On 2nd September *The Daily Telegraph* was able to give its readers the following information:

The agreement for exchange of contracts for the 'on-off-on' Theatre Museum project in the Old Flower Market, Covent Garden, was signed yesterday between the Government's Property Services Agency and the Greater London Council. Conversion of the 35,000 sq. ft. premises will take two years. The museum is expected to open to the public in 1986. A £250,000 donation from an anonymous source – believed to be the Rayne Foundation set up by Lord Rayne, the National Theatre Chairman – has made it possible for the previously postponed scheme to go ahead in the present financial year . . .

Once again a crisis had been weathered and on Monday, 30th January 1984, work started on the conversion of the Flower Market building.

17 Picasso design for costume worn by Massine as the Chinese Conjuror in the original production of the Diaghilev Ballet Russe *Parade* in Paris 1917. This ballet, with libretto by Jean Cocteau, music by Satie and choreographed by Massine, marked the painter's début as a stage designer. Bought by the Theatre Museum at auction in 1983. The Theatre Museum now has the original costume, bought with the generous help of Serge Lifar and Countess Ahlefeldt.

16 Serge Pavlovitch Diaghilev (1872–1929). This photograph (which originally included Jean Cocteau arm-in-arm with Diaghilev) will already be familiar to anyone interested in the Ballets Russes, which Diaghilev created. He was averse to being photographed and few portraits of him exist. Given by Nadia Nerina to the Friends of the Museum of Performing Arts.

18 The 'Magic piano' from *Salad Days*, the musical comedy with book and lyrics by Dorothy Reynolds and Julian Slade and music by Julian Slade. Originally staged at the Bristol Old Vic, it transferred to the Vaudeville Theatre, London, in August 1954, where it enjoyed a successful run of 2,283 performances. From the British Theatre Museum Collection.

19 The great Australian soprano Joan Sutherland in the mad scene from Donizetti's opera *Lucia di Lammermoor,* in the revival staged at the Royal Opera House, Covent Garden, 1959. Production, sets and costumes were by Franco Zeffirelli. Conducting on the first night, 17th February, was the veteran Italian opera conductor, Tullio Serafin. Photographed in performance by Houston Rogers, FRPS, FIIP. The huge collection of opera and ballet photographs, mostly taken during performances as distinct from photo calls, was acquired by the Theatre Museum after his death. The work of Houston Rogers covered, among other productions, most of the operas and ballets at the Royal Opera House, Sadler's Wells and the Festival Ballet.

20 Leon Bakst design, dated 1913, for the character of Likenion in the Diaghilev ballet *Daphnis and Chloë,* and worn by Mlle Shollar. In a later production the English ballerina Lydia Sokolova wore the same costume when dancing the leading role of Chloë. Diaghilev was not against ringing the changes in the ballet wardrobe for economic or other reasons. One of Bakst's original designs forming part of the collection of the Friends of the Museum of Performing Arts.

21 Ernest Van Dyck, the Belgian tenor, as the hero of Richard Wagner's last opera, *Parsifal,* in the 1888 production at the Festival Play-house, Bayreuth. Seen with him are the six soprano flower maidens of Klingsor, the Magician, in The Magic Garden. Gustave Kobbé describes the scene: 'Parsifal, attracted by the grace and beauty of the girls, leaps down into the garden and seeks to mingle with them. The girls, seeing that he does not seek to harm them, bedeck themselves with flowers and crowd around him as they sing.' But Parsifal is not to be tempted. The first performance of the opera, composed when Wagner was sixty-eight, was given at Bayreuth in 1882.

22 Clock-case commemorating the performance of Andrew Ducrow, specifically his representation of 'The Courier of St Petersburgh', the act which he invented in 1827. Antony Hippisley Coxe says: 'The scene is supposed to portray the journey of a courier on his way to Russia, the horses which pass beneath him representing the countries over which he must travel.' Ducrow used nine horses in this act. Besides being a talented mime and an actor on the legitimate stage, Ducrow was also animal trainer, contortionist, equilibrist, tight-rope dancer, choreographer and costume designer. He managed Astley's Amphitheatre in London and directed a number of the spectacles seen there between 1825 and 1841. The clock-case, made in rosewood with brass overlaid, is from the British Theatre Museum collection. The clock-face was added later.

23 An eighteenth-century pen-and-wash design by a member of the Galli da Bibiena family, depicting a terrace overlooking a garden. One of the thousands of items in the collection of playbills posters, newspaper cuttings, prints (some of these dating back to Caracci etchings published in 1591), Commedia dell'Arte engravings, eighteenth-century mezzotints, nineteenth-century lithographs, drawings, oil paintings and English satirical engraving which was the life work of Harry R. Beard. The collection, much of it amassed during Beard's European travels as a correspondent of *The Times* newspaper, was the source of many illustrations for Italy's monumental *Enciclopedia dello Spettacolo*. Formerly housed at Little Eversden near Cambridge, the Harry R. Beard Theatre Collection was presented to the Enthoven Collection on his death by the executors of his estate, in 1971.

24 'Bolton sheeting and rabbit' was Ellen Terry's description of the costume she wore for the mad scene when she played Ophelia to Irving's Hamlet at the Lyceum in 1878 – her first appearance with Irving. She had chosen to wear black in this scene, but when the veteran actor Walter Lacy, by then adviser to Irving on his Shakespearean productions, asked her if this was really her intention, she in turn asked him 'Why not?' '*Why not!* My God! Madam, there must be only one black figure in this play and that's Hamlet!' 'I did feel a fool', she wrote in *The Story of my Life,* 'What a blundering donkey I had been not to see it before!' She was worried because the black dress had involved the company in needless expense, 'So instead of *crêpe de chine* and miniver which had been used for the black dress, I had for the white dress Bolton sheeting and rabbit.' The material 'could not have cost more than two shillings a yard, and not many yards were wanted, as I was at that time thin to vanishing point.' When the collections acquired by the British Theatre Museum became part of the Theatre Museum many relics of this much loved actress became part of the archives. Photograph by Window & Grove.

25 Marie Malibran in the Prison Scene from the Beethoven opera *Fidelio.* By J. Absolon 1836. From the Enthoven Collection.

26 Alexandra Danilova (1904–), Russian-American dancer and teacher. A Soviet State dancer engaged by Diaghilev for his Ballets Russes when she was touring Western Europe in 1924. Seen here in the title-role of *Firebird,* ballet choreographed by Fokine with music by Stravinsky, costume designed by Goncharova, photographed by Anthony is mid 1930s. Gordon Anthony, famous internationally as a photographer of ballet dancers and author of more than a dozen photographic books on ballet. His sister, Dame Ninette de Valois, was founder of the Vic-Wells Ballet and the Royal Ballet. The Anthony Collection was acquired for the Enthoven Collection, and is now part of the Theatre Museum.

27 John Gielgud's four-star production of *Romeo and Juliet* at the New Theatre (now the Albery), 17th October 1935, made theatre history when Gielgud and Laurence Olivier alternated in the parts of Romeo and Mercutio. Edith Evans played the Nurse. The Juliet (not shown) was one of Peggy Ashcroft's loveliest portrayals. Sets and costumes were by Motely. In this photograph from the Debenham Collection, an important archive acquired by the British Theatre Museum, Olivier is seen in the character of Romeo and Gielgud as Mercutio.

29 Henry Irving in the title-role of *King Arthur,* Lyceum Theatre, 1895. Play adapted by Comyns Carr from Tennyson, with scenery and costumes designed by Sir Edward Burne-Jones (1833–98). Water-colour by Bernard Partridge. From the Harry R. Beard Theatre Collection.

28 Vaslav Nijinsky as the faun. This plaster original of the bronze cast by Una Troubridge was found in a London bookshop in 1954 by the English dancer Lydia Sokolova. In spite of its label 'Straight from the Temple of Mithras, 10s' (a topical reference to the excavations being carried out in the city at the time), Madame Sokolova recognized the likeness, and purchased the head. Later she agreed to four bronze casts being made. One of these is now in the Lincoln Center, New York; two are in private hands and the fourth belonged to Richard Buckle, who put it up for sale at Sotheby's in 1975, the proceeds going to the Acquisition Fund. It was purchased for £5,000. Richard Buckle presented the plaster head to the Theatre Museum. The ballet *L'Après-midi d'un Faune,* choreographed by Nijinsky, with music by Debussy and sets by Leon Bakst, was first staged by Diaghilev in Paris in the spring of 1912, when it created a sensation. The ballet was brought to London for the summer season that year and put on at Covent Garden, where, according to Anatole Hourman, 'Sir Thomas Beecham or Eugene Goossens held the baton at Diaghilev's invitation.'

31 Sarah Bernhardt (1845–1923) in *La Dame aux Camélias* by Alexandre Dumas the younger. Mrs Enthoven wrote of the great tragedienne: 'Sarah was an actress and gloried in the fact. All she did on the stage was thought out. I have seen her come off the stage having done a scene that has torn our hearts to ribbons and say, at her exit, that she would have "a not too much cooked entrecôte directly".'
From the Guy Little Collection of 17,000 historic theatrical photographs in the Enthoven Collection.

30 Caricature of actress Gertrude Lawrence by Einar Nerman, *c.*1945. Nerman's work was a regular feature in *The Sketch*. Gertrude Lawrence (1898–1952) started her career in pantomime when she was twelve years old and went on to a successful career as a dancer and leading-lady in revue. Later she appeared in many plays, including Noël Coward's *Private Lives*, 1930.
Presented by the artist's wife to the Theatre Museum.

33 Marie Taglioni (1804–84) as Flore in *Zéphire et Flore, c.*1834. Lithograph by R.J. Lane, ARA, from a drawing by A.E. Chalon, RA. One of the prints illustrating the Romantic Ballet presented, after the death of her husband playwright Ashley Dukes, by Dame Marie Rambert, DBE. Taglioni was Italian, born in Stockholm, and made her début in Vienna in 1822.

32 Maria Piltz as the Chosen Maiden in *The Rite of Spring,* ballet choreographed by Nijinsky to music by Igor Stravinsky. Sketch by the young French artist Valentine Gross, first wife of Jean Hugo, grandson of Victor Hugo. One of the in-performance sketches which she made of Diaghilev Ballet stars Nijinsky, Karsavina and Nijinska at the Théâtre des Champs-Elysées in Paris in the years between 1909 and 1913. The sketch was given to Richard Buckle by Jean Hugo for the Museum of Performing Arts.

By His *Majesty's* Company of *Comedians,*

AT THE

Theatre Royal in *Drury-lane,*

This present *Saturday,* being the 10th of *January,*
Will be presented a Comedy in Five Acts, call'd

The Way to keep Him.

The PRINCIPAL CHARACTERS by

Mr. GARRICK,
Mr. YATES,
Mr. PALMER,
Mr. KING,
Mr. ACKMAN,
Mrs. YATES,
Mrs. DAVIES,
Mrs. BRADSHAW, Mrs. HIPPISLEY,
Mrs. CLIVE,
AND

Mrs. CIBBER.

With a NEW PROLOGUE to be spoke

By Mr. HOLLAND.

To which will be added

The Double Disappointment.

Boxes 5s.   Pit 3s.   First Gallery 2s.   Upper Gallery 1s.
Places for the Boxes to be had of Mr. VARNEY at the Stage-door.

‡‡ No Admittance behind the Scenes, nor into the Orchestra.

34 *The Way to Keep Him.* Among hundreds of thousands of playbills in the Enthoven Collection is this bill announcing a performance at the Theatre Royal, Drury Lane, in 1761. Garrick had made his first appearance at Drury Lane, and took over the management of the theatre in 1747, introducing many reforms, including the rule that audiences were not allowed behind the scenes. Mrs Cibber and Kitty Clive were among the players he recruited. Mrs Hippisley, whose name also appears on the bill, was an ancestress of Antony Hippisley Coxe, whose circus collection is now part of the Theatre Museum.

35 Sarah Siddons. A contemporary plaster cast of the original self-portrait bust, *c.*1790, modelled by Mrs Siddons. Formerly in the possession of her son, this life-size bust was found in an orchard garden in Kent with the documents supporting its provenance stuffed into the interior. It was purchased at auction and later acquired by the BTMA with a grant from the Radcliffe Trust. The cast measures 27.5 × 28 × 64cm.

36 Pauline Chase as Peter Pan. Of all the actresses to have played the title-role in Sir James Barrie's *Peter Pan,* the name that comes most readily to mind is that of Pauline Chase, who many believe to have created the part. Two other Peters preceded her: Nina Boucicault and Cecilia (Cissie) Loftus. Pauline Chase's long connection with the play began when she played First Twin at the Duke of York's Theatre in 1904. Two years later she was engaged by Charles Frohman to play the lead. From then she made the part her own and played 'The boy who never grew up' for over a thousand performances between 1906 and 1913 and then disappeared from the stage. Born in Washington, USA, on 20th May 1885, Pauline Chase came to England in 1901, so was twenty-six when she first played Peter Pan. A succession of leading English actresses have since played the part, including Fay Compton, Gladys Cooper and Jean Forbes-Robertson. More recently Dorothy Tutin made a memorable and moving Peter. Pauline Chase's costume, with thigh boots and wooden sword were given to the British Theatre Museum by her son, Mr Peter Drummond.

37 The Beatles in action. The cult of the Beatles that swept the Western world in the 1960s produced its own commercial side-effects, including these models of the four member team, which were sold in d.i.y. kits, manufactured by Revells, ready for assembly and painting by the buyer. The figures are only a few centimetres high but immediately recognizable as the lads from Liverpool whose compositions sold millions of discs throughout the world. From left to right (the order in which they appeared on stage) are Paul McCartney, George Harrison, Ringo Starr and John Lennon. The Theatre Museum began collecting Rock'n'Roll material before it became fashionable to preserve such artefacts and now has an impressive collection relating to pop music and its spectacle.

38 Scene from *Coriolanus* with J.P. Kemble, Theatre Royal, Drury Lane, 7th February 1789. Hand-coloured mezzotint from the Harry R. Beard Theatre Collection.

39 Maria Meneghini Callas (1923–77) in the title-role of *La Traviata* by Giuseppe Verdi, Royal Opera House, Covent Garden, June 1958. Words by Francesco Maria Piave from the play *La Dame aux Camélias* by Alexandre Dumas the younger. Nicola Rescigno conducted the five performances of the opera sung by Callas at Covent Garden that season. The Musical Director was Rafael Kubelik; scenery and costumes of Sophie Fedorovitch. This photograph shows the great operatic soprano in the costume she wore in Act III, and is one of 45,000 photographs in the Houston Rogers Collection acquired by the Theatre Museum.

40 Costume design for *Balustrade* by Pavel Tchelitchev. Among ballet costumes in the collection of the Friends of the Museum of Performing Arts at the Theatre Museum are seven used in George Balanchine's *Balustrade*. This original ballet, with music by Igor Stravinsky and costumes and scenery by Tchelitchev, was premiered at the 51st Street Theatre, New York, 22nd January 1941. Although achieving only three performances – perhaps it was too erotic for the time – the ballet pleased the composer, who declared that it was 'one of the most satisfactory visualizations of any of my theatre works . . . a dance dialogue in perfect co-ordination with the dialogues of the music' (i.e. Stravinsky's Concerto in D for violin and orchestra).

The costume illustrated, described as 'The Jewel Girl' and worn by Tamara Toumanova, came up for sale at Sotheby's in December 1968, and it is thanks to the expert knowledge of Philip Dyer, now Ballet and Dance Consultant to the Theatre Museum, that this and the six other *Balustrade* costumes owe their positive identification. The costumes were made by Barbara Karinska, Russian-born *couturière,* famous from the 1930s to the mid-1970s, who worked closely with Balanchine on many of his ballets. Karinska is considered to have been not only a brilliant *couturière* but an intuitive interpreter of designs for ballet costumes. 'The Jewel Girl' is highly characteristic of her work. The four-movement ballet *Balustrade* had no plot, and got its name from the décor, which featured a white balustrade in the background. Toumanova appeared with Roman Jasinsky and Paul Petroff in a *pas de trois* in Aria, the third movement, and with the full cast in Capriccio, the final movement.

41 Front cloth after a gouache by Pablo Picasso for the Diaghilev ballet *Le Train Bleu,* called by Diaghilev 'a one-act *operette dansée',* and first performed in Paris in 1924. The cloth was purchased at Sotheby's sale at the Scala Theatre, London, in July 1967, for £69,000, with a grant from Lord Grade.

Georges Auric had been asked by Diaghilev to write a special fanfare to introduce the appearance of the cloth, which Diaghilev had Picasso's permission to enlarge and copy. Prince Shervashidze painted the cloth overnight in a studio off Tottenham Court Road, and succeeded so well that, according to Richard Buckle, Picasso 'Overcome with joy and admiration, inscribed Shervashidze's work in the bottom left-hand corner "Dedié à Diaghilev. Picasso"', thus confirming the authenticity of the fake.'

Le Train Bleu was choreographed by Nijinska, sister of Vaslav Nijinsky, to the music of the French composer Darius Milhaud. The decor was by Henri Laurens, the costumes by Coco Chanel and the story by Jean Cocteau, who got his inspiration for the ballet while watching Anton Dolin practising exercises in acrobatic technique. In her choreography Nijinska used movements connected with beach games, swimming, tennis and golf. The British ballerina Lydia Sokolova (born Hilda Munnings) created the part of Perlouse; Dolin was Beau Gosse and Leon Woizikowsky the Jouer de Golf.

42 Dame Adeline Genée, Danish-born prima ballerina of the Empire Theatre, Leicester Square, in Edwardian days, first danced in London in 1897. Thanks to her, Londoners came to accept ballet as a serious art-form again. After her retirement she devoted herself to the Royal Academy of Dancing, becoming its first President in 1920 and remaining in that office for the next thirty-four years. C. Wilhelm designed this costume for her when she appeared as Mlle Prevost in *La Danse* in 1914.

13 Master Betty – 'The Young Roscius'. The first entry in Acquisition Book, Vol I, on 20th May 1958, by G.B.L. Wilson, Hon. Curator of the British Theatre Museum, reads: 'Medal of W.H.W. Betty (1804)'. The medal, in white metal, by T. Webb bears the inscription 'The Young Roscius' on the obverse and on the reverse 'Not yet mature yet matchless. Born Septr. 16th 1791' and the date MDCCCIV. It was one of seven different medals struck to celebrate the phenomenal success of the boy actor. Master Betty was only thirteen years old when he reduced fashionable London audiences to a state bordering on mania with his portrayals of Hamlet and other major adult roles during one triumphant season from 1804 to 1805. Heralded after a provincial tour as 'The Tenth Wonder of the World', 'The Infant Roscius' and 'Garrick Reborn', this unknown Ulster-born lad filled the two Patent Theatres – Covent Garden and Drury Lane – almost to suffocation point, receiving £50 a night for his performances. Betty's promoters had done their work well and on 1st December, when he was due to open as the slave Achmet in *Barbarossa* (a version of Voltaire's *Mérope*) the crowds in Bow Street were so great that the military were called out to clear the approaches to the theatre, and only just prevented a catastrophe. During the performance, it is said that 'swooning persons of both sexes had to be dragged out of the human mass every few minutes'. Society, including the Prince of Wales, Lady Caroline Lamb, William Pitt and Charles James Fox, fell temporarily under Master Betty's spell, although it is evident that he was no more than a clever boy exploited by an unscrupulous father, who taught him every inflexion and every movement, and later, it is said by some, squandered his hard-earned money. Acclaim was short-lived and Master Betty was hissed off the stage when he appeared in Shakespeare's *Richard III*. After three years at Cambridge University he made an unsuccessful attempt at a come-back in 1811. The rest of his long life (he was over eighty when he died) was passed in obscurity. (See also no. 59 *The Theatrical Caesar*.)

44 'The Favourite Comic Dance'. Grimaldi. Coloured engraving from the Stone Collection in the Theatre Museum.

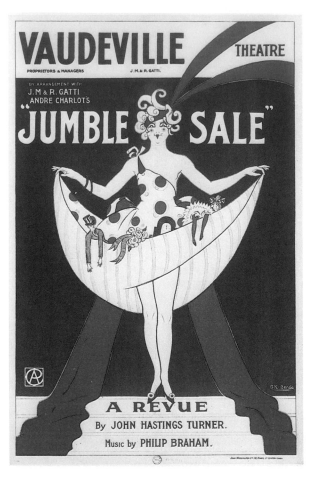

45 Theatre Poster by G.K. Benda for a revue, *Jumble Sale,* by John Hastings Turner, with music by Philip Braham, presented at the Vaudeville Theatre, 1920. From the Enthoven Collection.

46 Marie Lloyd (1870–1922), highly popular music-hall comedienne. Among her best-known numbers were *O, Mr Porter!, My Old Man Said Follow the Van* and *I'm One of the Ruins that Cromwell Knocked Abaht a Bit.* From the Guy Little Collection.

47 Henry Irving as Hamlet, after the painting by Edwin Long, RA. Irving played the part with outstanding success in his first Lyceum season, which opened on 30th December 1878. The painter and his wife were among the other guests when Irving went on a Mediterranean cruise in the steamer *Walrus,* chartered by the Baroness Burdett Coutts in the summer of 1879 at the end of that triumphal season. From the Harry R. Beard Theatre Collection.

48a 48b Silver cruet set in the likeness of the pantomime clown Joseph Grimaldi, 1778–1837. Grimaldi was the son of Giuseppe Grimaldi, ballet-master at Drury Lane. Joseph's career began at the age of three, when he appeared at Sadler's Wells Theatre. He created the only English member of the Harlequinade, and was a dancer, singer of comic songs and an acrobat. Acrobatics were his downfall and led to the end of his career. After his retirement in 1828 he wrote his memoirs, which were edited by Charles Dickens. The cruet set, in eight pieces, is from the Harry R. Beard Theatre Collection.

50 St George and the Dragon, mid-nineteenth century tinsel print from the Stone Collection.

49 The young French ballet dancer Emma Livry (1842–63), who studied under Marie Dominique and then became a pupil and protegée of the great Marie Taglioni, who saw in Emma a possible successor to herself. In 1861 Taglioni produced for her a ballet – *Le Papillon* – with music by Offenbach. A year later, during a rehearsal for a new production of the ballet *Le Muette de Portici* her costume caught fire and she died of her burns eight months later at the early age of twenty. Hard-paste porcelain figure (height 43cm), probably modelled by Auguste Barre in 1861; cast in Paris. From the Cyril Beamont collection.

51 *Massine waiting for his cue*, oil painting by Gluck, 1926. Gluck was the name used by a talented woman artist (1895–1978), only daughter of Joseph Gluckstein, one of the founders of J. Lyons & Co. From the British Theatre Museum Collection.

52 Costume for Hercules in Lully's *Tragédie Lyrique, Atys,* 1676, by Jean Bérain (1640–1711), French theatrical designer. Water-colour acquired by the Theatre Museum in 1982.

53 Vivien Leigh as 'Paola' and Claire Bloom as 'Lucile' in *Duel of Angels*, Apollo Theatre, London, 1958. The play, translated by Christopher Fry from the French of Jean Giraudoux, was directed by Jean-Louis Barrault, with décor by Roger Furse. Vivien Leigh is wearing one of the costumes designed for her by Christian Dior, which, with their accessories, were presented to the British Theatre Museum by Doris Langley Moore, Creator of the Costume Museum, Bath, and are now in the Theatre Museum.

Photograph by Angus McBean

54 Oliver Messel model set for Rossini's opera *Comte Ory* (Act I: outside the castle in Turin), Glyndebourne, August 1954. One of the items in the collection of Messel material presented to the Theatre Museum on indefinite loan by his nephew, Lord Snowdon, formerly President of the BTMA.

55 Stage design by Alexandre
Benois (1870–1960) for Acts I and II
of the ballet *Le Pavillon d'Armide.*
With scenario and décor by Benois,
music by Tcherepnine, choreography
by Fokine, the ballet was first performed by Diaghilev Ballets Russes
at the Théâtre du Châtelet, Paris,
19th May 1909. Its first production
was at the Marinsky Theatre, St
Petersburg, 1907. A member of a
Russian family with theatre associations going back many years,
Benois' best work was done for
Diaghilev. Purchased by the Theatre
Museum with funds generously provided by Sir Max Rayne.

56 The interior of Covent Garden Theatre when fire broke out at the conclusion of a *bal masqué* on 5th March 1856. The blaze sent the company rushing into the streets at 4 am. The building was totally destroyed and the loss of property estimated at more than £250,000. Coloured engraving from the Harry R. Beard Theatre Collection now part of the Theatre Museum.

57 Stage design in gouache by Sean Kenny for *The Hostage*, by Brendan Behan; play produced by Joan Littlewood, Stratford East, 1958. One of the many original designs formerly owned by the British Council and now deposited with the Theatre Museum.

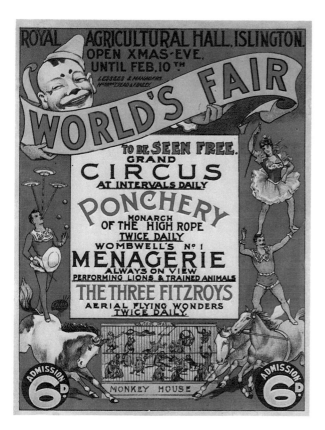

59 An example of English satirical engraving in the nineteenth century is this hand-coloured etching published in 1804 by F.E. Fores – one of many others in the Harry R. Beard Theatre Collection. Its publication coincided with Master Betty's phenomenal season at the Theatre Royal Drury Lane and the Theatre Royal Covent Garden. It shows John Philip Kemble (1757–1823), brother of Mrs Siddons, and his brother Charles Kemble (1775–1854), father of Fanny Kemble, as 'Cassius' and 'Casca' in debate on *The Theatrical Caesar*, i.e. William Henry West Betty.

58 Circus poster, Royal Agricultural Hall, Islington. From an early stage in its evolution it was agreed that the Theatre Museum should include material from every branch of the performing arts, the circus not excepted. In 1975 it acquired, on generous terms, the vast quantity of artefacts collected worldwide during thirty years by Antony Hippisley-Coxe. A further important collection of circus material, relating to the famous annual Bertram Mills Circus staged at Olympia, London, has since been acquired from his son Cyril Mills.

61 Juliet and the Nurse in the garden of Capulet's house. Stage design by Motley for the Glen Byam Shaw production of *Romeo and Juliet,* Shakespeare Memorial Theatre, Stratford-on-Avon 1958, in which Dorothy Tutin was the Juliet and Angela Baddeley the Nurse. Motley was the name adopted by three talented women designers, Margaret Harris and her sister Sophia Devine and Elizabeth Montgomery. 'Discovered' by John Gielgud in 1932, the Motleys quickly achieved fame both in this country and in the United States of America. For this production Margaret Harris designed the settings, Sophia Devine the costumes. One of a collection of original stage designs now deposited with the Theatre Museum by the Arts Council of Great Britain.

60 As part of its policy to represent all branches of the performing arts, the Theatre Museum is building up a collection of music-hall material. This costume design by Umberto Brunelleschi, 'Schéhérazade', *c.*1930, was purchased at a sale of ballet, theatre and music-hall items held at Sotheby's in October 1981. The design is executed in pencil, watercolour and gouache, is titled and signed and typical of the costumes used in the elegant and spectacular revues staged in Paris from the 1880s at the Théâtre des Folies-Bergère in the rue Richer.

62 Ellen Terry (1847–1928) in the title-role of *Dora*, drama by Charles Reade from the poem by Alfred, Lord Tennyson, Adelphi Theatre, 1878. From the Tom Taylor Collection presented to the British Theatre Museum by his daughter-in-law, Mrs Wycliffe Taylor, in 1965, now in the Theatre Museum.

63 Costume design by Michael Bronze for an ice show *c.*1968. Pencil and water-colour. These designs were witty parodies of Cecil Beaton's Ascot scene costumes from *My Fair Lady*. From the collection of costume designs given to the Theatre Museum in 1979 by Mrs Olive C.E. Austin.

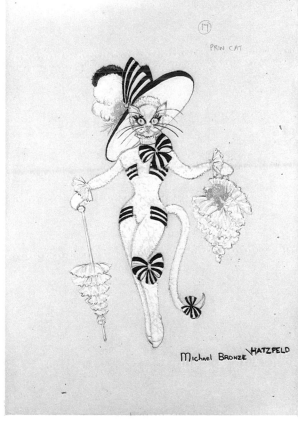

64 The Chosen Maiden and the Sage from *The Rite of Spring,* Diaghilev Ballet Russe, choreographed by Vaslav Nijinsky to music by Stravinksy, with scenery and costumes by Nicholas Roerich, first performed at the Théâtre des Champs-Elysées, Paris, May 1913. Two of the costumes exhibited in the spectacular 'Spotlight' exhibition staged by the Theatre Museum at the Victoria and Albert Museum, April 1981.

65 Playbill for Royal Command Performance at Windsor Castle, 25th January 1849. From the Enthoven Collection.

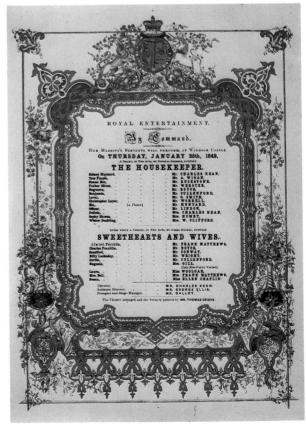

66 Satin programme for a Gala Performance at the Royal Opera House, Covent Garden, by command of His Majesty the King (Edward VII) in honour of the visit of the President of the French Republic on 7th July 1903. From the Enthoven Collection.

67 H.M. Brock poster for D'Oyly Carte Opera Company's production of *Iolanthe*, Princes Theatre, London 20th October 1919. From the Enthoven Collection.

69 George Grossmith (1848–1912) as the Lord Chancellor in *Iolanthe* by Gilbert and Sullivan, D'Oyly Carte Company production, Savoy Theatre, 25th November 1882. From the Enthoven Collection.

68 Japanese costume designed by C. Wilhelm, 1885. Wilhelm, born William Pitcher, 21st March 1858, was a designer, ballet-inventor, artist and self-trained draughtsman, who started work designing for the theatre in the 1870s and was responsible for 'costume effects' in more than a hundred plays. He used the name Wilhelm 'for family reasons'. From the Enthoven Collection.

Staged by the BTMA at the Saville Theatre, Shaftesbury Avenue,
London, prior to 1963:
Edward Gordon Craig, C.H., R.D.I. A Tribute offered by the BTMA
Hamlet 1874–1939
The Murray Carrington-Carmen Pedro Collection
Glamorous Nights the Musical Plays of Ivor Novello, and to
commemorate the Silver Jubilee of *Glamorous Night.*
'Punch' in the Theatre

**Staged by the BTMA at Leighton House (in addition to the opening
display in June 1963):**

Wars of the Roses – Material from the Royal Shakespeare Company's production at the Aldwych Theatre, 1963-	January 1964
Hamlet – Material from the opening production of the National Theatre at the Old Vic Theatre in 1963.	Spring 1964
Marie Tempest – Centenary.	July 1964
Mrs Patrick Campbell – Centenary.	January 1965
Ellen Terry and Her Family	June 1965
Sixty Years at the Aldwych	November 1965
Charles Ricketts and the Theatre	April 1966
Costumes, Portraits and Theatricalia – In conjunction with the Royal Borough of Kensington and Chelsea.	August 1966
Sixty Thousand Nights – The bi-centenary of the Theatre Royal, Bristol.	November 1966
Recent Acquisitions – Mounted by Philip Dyer.	May 1967
Adeline Genée – To mark Dame Adeline's 90th birthday. Mounted by Philip Dyer.	January 1968
Ellen Terry – In conjunction with Heinemanns, and to mark the publication of a biography by Roger Manvell.	April 1968
Sir Donald Wolfit's Bequest	August 1968
10th Anniversary of The Mermaid Theatre	May 1969
The Society for Theatre Research 21 Years, and Costumes for the Diaghilev Ballet – Mounted by Philip Dyer.	December 1969
The Royal Alexandra Theatre, Toronto	June 1970

October 1970	*Recent Acquisitions, including the Elizabeth Robbins Collection*
April 1971	*Ellaline Terris* – Centenary.
November 1971	*Rachel in London*
May 1972	*Edward Gordon Craig: The Early Years* – Centenary.
November 1972	*The Bells* – Material from the Russell-Cotes Art Gallery and Museum, Bournemouth.
September 1973	*Important Acquisitions from the Museum's Collections* – To celebrate the 10th Anniversary of its opening at Leighton House.

Staged by the Theatre Museum at the Victoria and Albert Museum and elsewhere:

March 1975	*Gilbert and Sullivan* – To coincide with the centenary of the D'Oyly Carte Company. Arranged by George Nash.
Summer 1975	*As Worn By . . .* – Held at the Salisbury Festival of the Arts, at the Guildhall, Salisbury, in association with the Theatre Museum: Designer: Richard Buckle with Philip Dyer (Wardrobe Master).
December 1975	*The Making of the Wombles* – Christmas Exhibition. Presented in association with the British Broadcasting Corporation and Film Fair Ltd.
January 1976	*Diaghilev Ballet Costumes* – At Leighton House. Arranged by Philip Dyer.
March 1976	*Theatre Peepshow* – At the National Theatre. Designed by John Ronayne, arranged by Janet Steen and Jennifer Aylmer.
March 1976	*200th Anniversary of the Burgteater, Vienna* – Presented for the Austrian Institute.
May 1976	*The Ballet Rambert* – Fifty years of memorabilia from the Ballet Rambert. Retrospective exhibition arranged by Philip Dyer.
July 1976	*Theatrical Caricatures by Einar Nerman* – Presented with the Messrs. George Harrap. At Leighton House.
August 1976	*The Richard Wagner Non-Stop Ring Show* – A continuous performance of the Decca recording and an exhibition of *The Ring* in England and Scotland. Arranged by Alexander Schouvaloff.
October 1976	*Jean Hugo Designs for the Theatre* – From the collection of the artist.
December 1976	*Hoffnung's World of Music* – Mrs Annetta Hoffnung's collection of her husband's drawings.
May 1977	*Harley Granville Baker* – At the National Theatre. Centenary of his birth. Designed by John Ronayne; arranged by Margery Morgan.
May 1977	*Royal Box* – Coinciding with the Silver Jubilee of HM The Queen. A tribute to over 400 years of royal patronage of the theatre. Designed by Bruno Santini.
November 1977	*Revudeville* – The story of the Windmill Theatre. Arranged by Janet Steen. Designed by John Ronayne.
May 1978	*Adeline Genée* – Centenary. A pictorial record by Ivor Guest. Arranged by Philip Dyer.
August 1979	*Parade* – Edinburgh Festival Diaghilev Ballet Exhibition. At Edinburgh College of Art. Designed by John L. Paterson.

*Publication

†*Spotlight* – Four Centuries of Ballet Costume, including a Tribute to the   April 1981
Royal Ballet. Designed by John L. Paterson. Display by Philip Dyer and
Judith Doré.

Silk Stars of the Theatre Museum – At Liberty, Regent Street. Display   September 1982
by Philip Dyer and Sarah C. Woodcock.

†*Show Business* – Coinciding with the Theatre Museum publication   November 1982
Images of Show Business, edited by James Fowler. Arranged by James
Fowler and Janet Steen.

†*A Month in the Country* – Arranged by April FitzLyon and Alexander   May 1983
Schouvaloff.

†*Oliver Messel* – From the collection of Lord Snowdon. Organized by   June 1983
Roger Pinkham and Leela Meinertas.

Scenery from the Diaghilev Collection and Costumes from The Sleeping   June 1983
Princess – at Olympia, London. In connection with the Fine Art and
Antiques' Fair. Display by Sarah C. Woodcock and Philip Dyer.

Photographs by Anthony, reprinted by Graham Brandon – At Sadler's   December 1983
Wells Theatre. Display by Sarah C. Woodcock and Philip Dyer.

Anton Dolin - 1964–1983 – Arranged by Sarah C. Woodcock and Leela   June 1984
Meinertas. Photography by Graham Brandon.

In addition to the exhibitions listed above, there were micro-exhibi-
tions at the Theatre Museum, Victoria and Albert Museum, including:

Micro Exhibitions

Othello – Arranged by Anne Tuckwell   August 1980

John Lennon – At the time of his death. Arranged by Danny Friedman.   December 1980

Royal Processions – To coincide with the wedding of HRH The Prince   July 1981
of Wales – Arranged by Anne Tuckwell.

Stravinksy rehearses Stravinsky – Centenary of his birth. Photographs   June 1982
by Laelia Goehr.

Ralph Richardson - 1902–1983. Arranged by Danny Friedman   January 1984

A Midsummer Night's Dream – Arranged by Naomi Joshi.   July 1984

† Catalogue

SELECT
BIBLIOGRAPHY

BAKER, H. Barton — *History of the London Stage and its Players, 1576–1903.* London, Routledge, 1904.

BUCKLE, Richard — *Diaghilev.* London, Weidenfield and Nicholson Ltd, 1979.

BUCKLE, Richard — *In the Wake of Diaghilev: Autobiography Two.* London, Collins, 1981.

DOBBS, Brian — *Master Betty.* London, Cassell & Co. Ltd, 1972.

COXE, Antony Hippisley — *A Seat at the Circus.* With special illustrations by John Skeaping. Revised Edition. London, Macmillan, 1980.

HOURMAN, Anatole — *The Tragedy of Nijinsky.* London, Robert Hale Ltd, 1937.

IRVING, Laurence — *Henry Irving: The Actor and His World.* London, Faber and Faber, 1951.

KOBBÉ, Gustave — *Complete Opera Book.* Edited and revised by the Earl of Harewood. London, Putnam, 1976.

KOEGLER, Horst — *The Concise Oxford Dictionary of Ballet.* O.U.P., 1977.

LAVER, James — *Museum Piece or the Education of an Iconographer.* London, André Deutsch Ltd, 1963.

MANVELL, Roger — *Sarah Siddons – Portrait of an Actress.* London, Heinemann Group of Publishers Ltd, 1970.

MUSEUMS JOURNAL, The — *Proceedings of the public meeting held at the Arts Council, 28.10.55.* London, 9.12.55.

NORWICH, The Viscount — *The British Theatre Museum.* Journal of the Royal Society of Arts, July 1968.

PLAYFAIR, Giles — *The Prodigy.* London, Secker and Warburg Ltd, 1967.

ST. JOHN-STEVAS, Norman — *The Two Cities.* London and Boston, Faber and Faber, 1984.

STONE, Professor George Winchester — *A Tribute to the British Theatre Museum.* Theatre Notebook, Winter 1964–5.

SAXON, A.H. — *The Life and Art of Andrew Ducrow.* Connecticut, U.S.A., Archon Books, 1978.

TREWIN, J.C. — *Edwardian Theatre, The.* Oxford, Basil Blackwell, 1976.

INDEX
(including biographical notes)